Kulshan.com's

GUIDE TO
Whatcom County

glen berry

Kulshan.com's Guide to Whatcom County By
Glen Berry

Foreword, Photography, and Chapter Introductions By
Glen Berry

Layout, Design and Production
Ruth Lauman

Copy Editor
Ken Brierly

Contributing Authors

Kimberly Baer
Glen Berry
Wayne Berry
Ken Brierly
Shelagh Considine
Dave Erickson
Debra Exley
Hilary Higgins
Beth Marsau
Rob Olason
Tanya Perkins
Dave Shepherd
Nancy Steele
Tyler Watson

Copyright (c) 1999 by Sign Me Up Marketing

FIRST EDITION

Our heartfelt appreciation to the authors who have worked so enthusiastically on their assignments. The high quality of the content contributed clearly demonstrates that there is no lack of talent in Whatcom County.

ISBN: 0-9674389-0-x

Manufactured in the United States of America

Table of Contents

RESTAURANTS

MEDITERRANEAN *(continued)*

FINE DINING

DRIVE-IN

ALTERNATIVE

COMMUNITY

GOVERNMENT

TRANSPORTATION

KID'S

PUBLIC SERVICE

LANDMARKS

LIBRARIES

Introduction

W hat you are about to read is a collection of write-ups on the most compelling and interesting places in Bellingham and Whatcom County, handpicked by local residents. They were chosen for their background and history, aesthetics, atmosphere, clientele and the importance to the community.

These write-ups were culled from Kulshan.com, Whatcom County's most popular Web site. This book is a reflection of Kulshan.com's collection of restaurant reviews, park profiles and outdoor destinations, as well as gallery and museum write-ups. The Web site has enjoyed enormous popularity since its launch, and has grown rapidly with the overwhelming support of the people of Whatcom County. As the site grew in depth and diversity, it was a natural step to put this extensive collection of information into the form of a book for people to enjoy away from their computers.

Although we applied stringent information guidelines to the locations we chose to cover, our highest priority was producing content that was reader-friendly. As we tell our writers, "Plain English is best — pretend you are explaining what it's about to a friend." Our goal was not to produce an esoteric work, but rather something that would be as down-to-earth and as accessible as the community it describes.

For those unfamiliar with this area, "Kulshan.com's Guide to Whatcom County" is nearly encyclopedic in its area documentation. Most residents will be familiar with many of the locations, but it is almost certain that each write-up contains some new information that readers will find intriguing. As the editor of Kulshan.com, I am always amazed with each new discovery about the community where I grew up. Even more surprising is that many of these places are often times right under our noses, something we pass by everyday, but don't really see.

The purpose of this book is to introduce the reader to hot, new places, little known favorites and serve as a reminder of long-time standbys. Each feature offers a description, address, driving instruction, contact information and an informative, straightforward profile.

Our motivation for creating this book — and Kulshan.com — is our focus on community. The suggestions for the locations came from the locals, choices of the locations were made by life-long residents and the writing itself was done by a diverse group of authors from all the communities within Whatcom County. The result is a wealth of knowledge and "insider" information created with area residents in mind.

The Fourth Corner has a unique identity from other areas in our region. Our goal has been to celebrate that distinction, and foster a sense of community by bringing all of this information together into one source. We hope you enjoy this book. It was made for you.

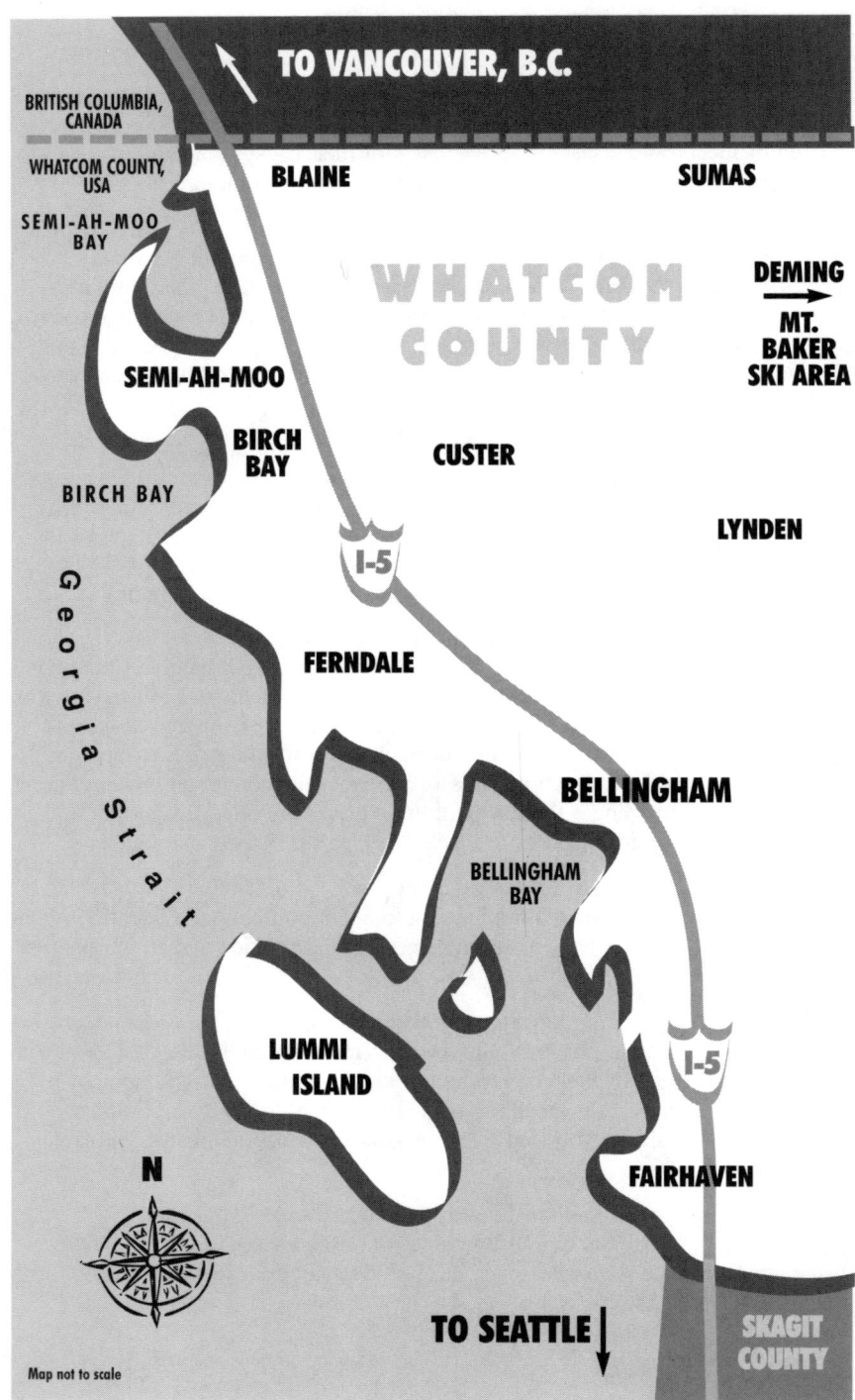

Outdoors

When asked about their reason for living in the Pacific Northwest, many people cite the natural surroundings – ocean, islands, rivers, mountains, hills and forests. Whatcom County certainly has all this to offer and in such abundance that outdoor enthusiasts can find trails and parks at every turn.

Bellingham is indeed unique in the amount of park area that it offers its inhabitants. With over 15 percent of the city's total land area utilized as a park or natural reserve, Bellingham leads the nation in the amount of "green space" available. An almost countless number of national, state, county and city parks in Whatcom County range from well-known and heavily trafficked waterfront destinations, to rugged and remote wilderness areas.

In addition, there are many unofficial "parks," trails and undeveloped areas for exploring, known only to a few avid joggers and neighborhood children. Perhaps the most delightful aspect of having so many parks and recreational areas at your disposal is the thrill of finding hidden paths and sections of woods that give the illusion of exploration and discovery. Not only this, but nature areas and parks are literally at your front door and can be accessed in minutes – not an hour's drive away through city traffic.

In the following section, we have made an effort to cover some of the most unique and popular of Whatcom County's outdoor opportunities. Although we have barely made a dent, there are plenty of great places described, so you can begin enjoying the natural beauty of the region.

Outdoors

Fairhaven Park

Address
107 Chuckanut Drive
Bellingham WA, 98225

Hours
Every day Dawn - Dusk

Directions:
South of the Fairhaven District on Chuckanut Drive.

Features
Basketball Courts, Walking Trails, Kid Friendly, Bathrooms

Description
Great bricked archways span the entrance to this 16 acre recreational reserve, located just minutes from the Fairhaven District on Chuckanut Drive. Inside, you'll find plenty of parking and well planned spaces that meet the needs of any group's athletic urges: swing sets, tennis courts, basketball hoops, and backstop, plus big yawning stretches of lawn to satisfy the unathletic urges as well. For *"les petites"* in the family, a nicely fenced wading pool is sure to delight.

The low rise of land slopes gradually upward, allowing you to take in nearly the entire expanse of park at a single glance. The impression conveyed in its upper regions is that of a graceful wooded estate. Northern margins intertwine with the Interurban trail network and give park users an additional site for strolling or dog walking. Kids will likely find the gentle stream and fallen trees in that section as absorbing as the park's play equipment.

Scattered picnic benches, many with grills, dot the grassy areas. You'll schlep your picnic goods a fair distance to some, but will be rewarded by the relative isolation. Packed gravel paths make transit possible for wheelchairs. Restrooms are accessible.
For special group events, three covered areas are available by reservation (Parks & Rec. Dept. 676-6985): a "Small Shelter" with sink & counter; a "Large Shelter" with water, lights, electricity and restrooms; and the enclosed "Pavilion", suitable for dressed up occasions, includes a full kitchen.

Facilities are extremely well maintained with grounds that are handsome and groomed. Fairhaven Park is a tribute to the community, its users and certainly the staff who oversee it's care. The spit and polish bearing of those bricked entry arches accurately reflect what you'll find once inside.

Written by Debra Exley

Clark's Point

Address
Southern End of Fieldston Road
Bellingham WA, 98225

Hours
Every day Dawn - Dusk

Directions:
From Fairhaven, head south on Chuckanut Drive. Turn right on
Viewcrest, at Fieldston turn left. There is public parking at
Fieldston and Arbutus.

Features
Kid Friendly, Walking Trails

Description
Clark's Point is really two short walking trails offering the casual
hiker two very different outdoor experiences.

On a warm summer day, the western trail takes you through a
forest of second growth Douglas Fir, Maple and Alder trees. In
the forest canopy above, the sounds of birds calling echo into
the distance. Along the trail, the sweet scent of blooming salmon
berry draws the occasional bee.

Climbing up one small rise, the trail terminates on the sandstone
bluff of Jones Point. The bluff is about thirty feet above Puget
Sound and offers a spectacular head-on view of Lummi Island.
Orcas Island and the rest of the San Juan Islands fan out to the
South and behind Lummi. On a clear day, the Olympic Mountains
to the South and the Canadian Cascades to the North add the
final touch to this great viewpoint.

A short but steep side trail on Jones Point brings you down
closer to the shore and the railroad tracks. At low tide a small
beach is exposed just below the bluff. The remainder of the
shoreline along the tracks is all large rock used to reinforce the
track bed and is home to crabs, starfish and other sea life.
A small man-made lagoon is on the other side of the tracks.

While the western trail primarily offers an incredible view of the
San Juans, if you visit Clark's Point with children, you'll find the
eastern trail provides more opportunities for youngsters to
explore. This short trail takes you to the Chuckanut Creek Estuary
which is the North end of Chuckanut Bay. Again the rail bed is a
prominent feature here—it's a World War I era causeway that cre-
ates a calm bay on its north side, dampening the effect of strong
winter storms, and providing a safe haven for sea life.

Children will enjoy the small beaches on either side of the track.
Further out on the causeway, an angler may be trying their luck,
casting out from the trestle, taking advantage of an incoming tide.
Be sure to check a tide timetable if you want to beach comb at
Clark's Point. Much of the beach is accessible only at low tide.
Each trail is only about a five minute walk, which is an amazingly
short journey to be transported into such a spectacular setting.

Written by Rob Olason

Elizabeth Park

Address
Holly Street & Eldridge Avenue
Bellingham WA, 98225

Hours
Every day Dawn - Dusk

Directions:
The park is located near the intersection of Holly Street,
Eldridge Avenue and Broadway by St. Paul's church.

Features
Bathrooms, Picnic Area

Description
Nestled within one of Bellingham's oldest neighborhoods lies
Elizabeth Park, the city's oldest municipal park. The homes in this
Victorian neighborhood are the same age as any of the walnut,
chestnut and big-leaf maple trees in the park — well over 100-
years old. The deciduous trees capture the nuances of any season:
budding leaves and blossoming shrubs in the spring, chestnuts
and walnuts falling to the ground in summer's shade, mounds of
fragrant and brittle leaves in the autumn and snow-lined silver
frost on the twisted, black bark of Elizabeth's trees in winter.

A fountain surrounded by benches is the centerpiece of the park
and a fairly large gazebo mimics the colors of the fallen leaves.
Elizabeth has two tennis courts and one paved basketball court.
Also, if the kids are too young to climb trees, they'll have fun on
the slides and swing-set. Aside from the winter months, Elizabeth
also has open restrooms.

As old as the park is, it is not particularly wheelchair accessible.
The park's perimeter is a paved sidewalk, but the paths within
the park are gravel trails. Elizabeth is, however, a great place to
picnic and the surrounding neighborhood is a great place to
roam and admire the ornate Victorian architecture.

Written by Ken Brierly

Larrabee State Park

Address
245 Chuckanut Dr.
Bellingham WA, 98227

Hours
Every day Dawn - Dusk

Directions:
To get to Larrabee, take 12th Street south from Old Fairhaven past Fairhaven Middle School and Fairhaven Park. Twelfth Street becomes Chuckanut Drive past Fairhaven Park and follow the road for seven miles. The park is on your right.

Features
Bathrooms, Picnic Area, Picnic Tables, Walking Trails

Description
Located off scenic Chuckanut Drive near the Whatcom/Skagit County border, Larrabee State Park offers a tidal and wooded wilderness just minutes south of Bellingham. Established in 1915 as Washington's first state park, Larrabee is also one of the largest — spanning 2,683 acres, from sea level to 1,940 feet elevation, and occupies most of the west side of Chuckanut Mountain.

Visitors to Larrabee may participate in various forms of recreation, including picnicking (67 picnic sites); boating (including a boat launch); fishing, clamming and crabbing (permits required); hiking (9.3 miles of trails); camping (53 standard sites, 8 walk-in and 26 trailer-hookup sites); water skiing and scuba diving. Larrabee also has an amphitheater, large fields and other day-use amenities. However, most people visit Larrabee to explore the beach — the rocky shoreline is famous for its many tide pools packed with aquatic life.

More adventurous types can hike a few miles up Chuckanut Mountain to Fragrance and Lost Lakes. The route up to these areas boasts three lookout sites featuring sweeping views of the San Juan Islands and Rosario Strait. Camping and fresh-water fishing is allowed at the lakes, but be sure to verify whether campfires are permitted at the time you visit and that anglers are carrying their fishing licenses.

Written by Ken Brierly

Outdoors

Blaine Marine Park

Address
Marine Drive
Bellingham WA, 98225

Hours
Every day Dawn - Dusk

Directions:
Head toward the railroad tracks on Marine Drive. Once you cross them , the park will be right there on your right, across the street from the Visitor's Information Center.

Features
Kid Friendly, Bathrooms, Picnic Tables, Biking Trails, Picnic Area, Walking Trails

Description
Blaine Marine Park sits overlooking the sea, the quaintest, most peaceful spot in all of Washington. Beneath a flowering tree is a bench that faces the rocky beach and, further out, the water. Sitting there, under the tree as its blossoms, pink and delicate, drip down on your shoulders, watching the toss of gray out beyond the beach, it is possible to feel as though you have accidentally fallen into a Bronte novel.

But if a picnic is all that's on the agenda, that's do-able too. The park has four picnic shelters, two with two tables each, two with one each, all reserveable. Uncovered and on top of a slight, grassy slope just big enough for a good game of tag, are five more picnic tables. Here, at the bottom of the slope, is the totem pole dedicated to the park by the Claymore family. Tall and alone, it is almost majestic.

If the Claymore's pole is majestic, the beach is simply spiritual. At low tide, you find you are walking on a carpet of shells, like a giant hand swept a huge clutch of them from the sea, crushed and then sprinkled them liberally over the sandy beach. When the grass is freshly mowed, the pungent aroma of salt and green is so earthy it's reverent. You might notice only in passing though, if you are busy at your family reunion on the Orca Platform or watching a play in the Amphitheater. Both are reservable, and both are clean and spacious enough for a variety of functions.

The Blaine Marine Park is a great spot for a walk on your lunch break, perfect for the yearly office picnic. Tidy and well-kept, it's ideal for hot dogs with your kids, family functions, awards ceremonies and the like. It's certainly worth the drive on a breezy Sunday afternoon.

Written by Holly Gray

Outdoors

Birch Bay State Park

Address
Helwig Road
Blaine WA, 98230

Hours
Closed on Christmas
6:30am - Dusk

Directions:
Take Exit 266 off the I-5 heading north from Bellingham. At the intersection, turn left and follow the clearly posted signs for Birch Bay State Park.

Features
Kid Friendly, Bathrooms, Picnic Tables, Walking Trails, Basketball Courts, Picnic Area, Swimming Areas

Description
Birch Bay State Park offers spectacular views of the San Juan Islands and the Canadian Rockies, and an opportunity to explore the shoreline, forests and marshes typical of the Pacific Northwest. In past centuries, Semiahmoo Indians fished and gathered edible plants from the park's shoreline. Captain George Vancouver is credited with discovering Birch Bay in 1792 and named the area for the plentiful trees he found. The nineteenth century saw the area become important to the logging industry; however, in 1954, the need to protect the natural beauty of the site was recognized and it became part of the state park system. Today, both day visitors and campers can enjoy the quiet forests, wetlands and curving shoreline of Birch Bay State Park, ideal for clamming, walking, swimming or just relaxing and enjoying the vista.

A important feature of the park is Terrell Marsh Trail, a one-half mile hiking trail through Puget Sound forest and marsh environments. Terrell Creek Marsh is one of the last saltwater/freshwater estuaries in this part of Washington. The self-guided interpretive trail offers an extremely beautiful meander through a typical northwest mixed forest, including a view of Terrell Marsh, home to blue herons, red-winged blackbirds and other water fowl. The trail has a slight slope and is a very easy walk, even for small children.

Located approximately 18 miles from Bellingham and 30 miles south of Vancouver, Canada, the park offers day use and camping facilities. Day use areas are located near the beach, and include picnic tables, fire pits, restrooms, a basketball court, a rain shelter and open grass for leisure activities. Parking is plentiful. The park's 167 campsites are fairly private, and sheltered by towering cedars and douglas firs. Utilities are available at some sites. For those who can't camp without roasting marshmallows, firewood is available from the campground concessionaire or from the local store located near the park entrance. The park is open year-round; reservations are recommended, with unreserved sites available on a first-come, first-served basis.

Written by Tanya Perkins

Pioneer Park

Address
2004 Cherry Street
Ferndale WA, 98248

Hours
Every day Dawn - Dusk

Directions:
Take the Ferndale 262 Exit and travel west. Turn left on 1st Avenue (the first street after crossing the Nooksack) and go to the end of the street.

Features
Bathrooms, Picnic Area, Picnic Tables, Kid Friendly, Baseball Diamonds

Description
Pioneer Park is the cornerstone of the City of Ferndale's system of parks and open spaces. Purchased by the Whatcom old Settlers Association in the late 1800's, the park was deeded to the City of Ferndale in 1972. The 25 acre park, located on the banks of the Nooksack River, features a children's play area, mature cedar trees, picnic shelters, softball fields and stage.

Pioneer Park represents one of the finest collections of original pioneer log cabins and artifacts in the world. The twelve log cabins sat alone in forests and rough clearings at locations throughout Whatcom County. Over the course of several decades the cabins were moved to the park by members of the Old Settlers Association, Ferndale Heritage Society and city to save them from destruction. One of the oldest buildings in the park, the Church, is a popular location for small weddings. Each cabin serves as a museum, packed with artifacts from around Whatcom County predating World War II.

The park hosts a variety of activities throughout the year. Guided tours of the cabins are available seasonally from May 15 through September 15. It is not uncommon to see antique car shows, children's day camps and concerts in the park on any given day during the summer. The last full weekend in July features the Old Settlers Picnic, one of the oldest running special events in the state. In December, the park is transformed into a winter wonderland for the Old Fashioned Christmas. With the aroma of fresh baked bread and cedar boughs and the sound of Christmas carols filling the air, this event will definitely put you in the holiday spirit. Whether you visit for the day or an hour, Pioneer Park is a place you won't want to miss.

Written by Dave Erickson

Semiahmoo Spit

Address
Semiahmoo Parkway
Blaine WA, 98230

Hours
Every day Dawn - Dusk

Directions:
Exit I-5 at the Lynden/Birch Bay exit and head west following the signs to Semiahmoo Park and The Inn at Semiahmoo.

Features
Biking Trails, Wheelchair Accessible, Picnic Tables

Description
A sweeping gaze from the Semiahmoo Spit takes in two countries, two mountain ranges, two bodies of water and the varied vessels that ply these Northern sound waters.

The full distance of this land finger is marked by a paved walking path, with natural grasslands flanking both sides. Shallow driftwood beaches rise up on either margin and lone tree snags stand watch to the comings and goings. The full mile of path can be strolled in a half hour, unless your stick-chasing dog slows you at water's edge. Bring your kayak for a flat paddle within the protected harbor or venture out into the chop of open bay waters. Bicycling is plentiful with some thigh burning hills close by or the welcomed flat lands of the spit's parkway.

Whatcom County's first salmon cannery was built on the Semiahmoo Spit in 1881. Ten years later, operating as the Alaska Packers Association, it was the largest of its kind in the world. A vestige of the cannery remains there today in company with the posh grounds of the Inn at Semiahmoo.

Road travel to the spit is over hill and dale and you'll be breezing by the waterslide enticements of Birch Bay. On summer weekends, consider taking the Plover, a passenger (and bicycle!) ferry that leaves from Blaine. It will plunk you right down on a wharf at spit's end. It's a fully restored ferry that was built in 1944 to shuttle Cannery workers over the brief passage of harbor waters. The vessel captain, a man born of the sea, lets kids take a hand at the wheel and then offers up a certificate for their helmsmanship.

On a sunny day, diamond sparkles dance on the waters of Semiahmoo Bay to the north and Drayton Harbor to the south. The spit of land carves a clean slice through their middle, affording its visitors a recreational perch for their day by the sea.

Written by Debra Exley

Berthusen Park

Address
8837 Berthusen Road
Lynden WA, 98264

Hours
Every day Dawn - Dusk

Directions:
Take the Bay-Lynden Road exit (270) off I-5 & head east for 7 miles then left on Berthusen Road to the park.

Features
Horseshoe Pits, Picnic Area, Walking Trails, Bathrooms, Picnic Tables, Wheelchair Accessible

Description
If pitching a tent or parking your RV amidst the cedar spires of an old growth forest sounds appealing, then the hearts' desire of Hans C. Berthusen has come full circle. These campgrounds are a portion of Berthusen Park, which stands as testimony to the industry and generosity of this early Whatcom homesteader. Hans Berthusen single-handedly cleared 100 acres of the densely forested land and then left twenty more of it in virgin timber for the sheer gladness of living amongst his trees. Upon his death in 1944, he left the entire 236 acres to the city of Lynden.

Extreme tidiness prevails throughout this well-managed park, where the forest floor practically looks swept. Twenty nine "standard" camp sites (with tables and fire pits) plus 24 "utility" sites (with power and water) are clustered throughout the enchanted forest. An RV dumping station is provided at the park exit. Restrooms have hot and cold water and flush toilets. Three covered shelters are available for group reservations. Playground equipment is scattered beneath the forest canopy and paths suitable for hikers or horses trail off into wooded areas. Of course, equestrians are asked to remove waste from the trails.

The real campground showpiece is the enormous barn Berthusen erected for farm equipment and livestock. Its great cavernous proportions are stunning. Shards of light filter through the planked walls of this 4 story high structure. If Hans ever hosted a barn dance, it could easily have been a global affair. Its immense interior miniaturizes the 50+ pieces of antique farm machinery and implements there for your viewing—they will make you forget what century you're in.

This unusually pleasant campground, minutes off I-5, won't let you get away without a final, parting smile. Posted for RV'ers at the park's exit: "Is your step up; antenna down, spouse with? Thanks, bye."

Written by Debra Exley

Big Rock Garden

Address
2900 Sylvan Street
Bellingham WA, 98226

Hours
Every day Dawn - Dusk

Directions:
Located in the Silver Beach Neighborhood, Big Rock Garden is on the north side of Alabama Street at 2900 Sylvan Street. You'll see the sign on the right near the top of the hill.

Features
Bathrooms, Picnic Tables

Description

As one of Bellingham's least-known parks, Big Rock Garden is also one of the most unique. The 2.7-acre garden is part of a 9.2-acre woodland overlooking Lake Whatcom. The garden is packed with an eclectic group of sculptures as well as native and exotic plants, trees and shrubs. A paved parking area provides access to the garden; inside the garden's fences, visitors will find a packed gravel path to direct them to the various sculptures, plants and landscaping marvels.

Big Rock Garden also has restrooms, a greenhouse and tool building. Stop and rest at the elevated deck area at the bottom of the garden. There, you may sit in benches or chairs and soak in a glimmering view of the lake and its surrounding hills. You may also walk through the woodland trail of the park. Located outside the garden's boundaries, walk east behind the water tower. The trail begins at the edge of the woods and winds through a mixed-growth forest for about a half-mile. A bench overlooking the lake is perched in the clearing at the trail's endpoint.

The city purchased the park in 1993 from the family of former city council member George Drake. The family created the garden in 1980 as a nursery and art sculpture gallery. The original intent was to create a small family business that could provide opportunities for mentally handicapped people. As the surrounding areas are developed, the park will become an island of forest on the Silver Beach skyline.

Written by Ken Brierly

Hovander Park

Address
5299 Neilson Rd.
Ferndale WA, 98248

Hours
Every day 8:00am - 9:00pm

Directions:
From Main St. in Ferndale, turn south onto Hovander. Take a right at Neilson Rd. and the park's entrance will be on your right.

Features
Picnic Tables, Kid Friendly, Horseshoe Pits, Bathrooms, Picnic Area

Description
When you visit Hovander Homestead Park, be prepared to spend a few hours. Such a vivid time travel experience will surely take up a Saturday afternoon. To be properly prepared, wear comfortable walking shoes and consider packing a picnic lunch and toting along the camcorder or Polaroid. There is a lot of ground to cover at Hovander, and much to see.

The park is extensive and well cared for. Home to horses, chickens, rabbits, pigs, goats and many more, Hovander is a veritable Old MacDonald's Farm. The animals are accessible, easy to view and, where appropriate, okay to feed. Beyond being almost a zoo, Hovander park was once the homestead of a Swedish family which immigrated to the United States. The house bears the markings of Swedish architecture, beautiful and quaint. Surrounded by lush gardens, prepared and maintained by master gardeners, the house seems to sit in a frame of purples, reds and azure. Inside, the Hovander home is rich with antiques and wordless history. Truly, the house is an educational, if not spiritual, experience.

Lawns surround the house and, next to it, a huge red barn. They are peppered with many picnic tables and grills. Absolutely perfect for a family reunion or Sunday afternoon lunch, there is even a small play area for children featuring a swing set, slide and a big red tractor. Just behind the playground is a wooden lookout tower. Climb to the top and you will get a spectacular view of the Hovander homestead, from the horse field to the barn to the house and down to the grove of trees that serves as a buffer between the park and the Nooksack river. It is clear from there, at the top of the tower, that Hovander park is a gift. A spread of green carpet, home to flowers and plants and animals of all sizes, the living representative of the Hovander family.

Written by Holly Gray

Outdoors

Bloedel Donovan

Address
2214 Electric Street
Bellingham WA, 98226

Hours
Every day Dawn - Dusk

Directions:
Drive east up Alabama Hill and turn right at the end of the street where it meets the lake. Turn left at the second entrance on the left.

Features
Bathrooms, Picnic Area, Picnic Tables

Description
You know the place — during the hottest days of summer, the journey to its cool waters requires one to first wade through a sea of treacherous, screaming, picnicking humanity. Seagulls and crows raid garbage cans and unguarded barbecue pits. A lifeguard perched high in a chair shouts a continuous stream of incoherent, yet loud, warnings at kids horsing around somewhere out on the docks. Jet skis and powerboats buzz around in the distance, as do crazy bees on a wood-stained deck. Finally you get there — into the most soothing, sky reflecting blue water. Ah, the public swimming hole. You know the place — Bloedel Donovan Park and Pavilion, located at the western-most end of Lake Whatcom.

Really, it's only that way for one month of the year. In reality, Bloedel's a pretty cool place. It is one of the few places in the city dog owners can let the mutts loose without having to anticipate that first glimpse of the animal control's hot-dog wagon and subsequent citation. Fido also has plenty of birds to chase. Above the lake and past the parking lot, Bloedel has one of the best soccer fields in the city — and what a location for it! After a grueling and muddy practice, nothing treats you better than a cool plunge off one of the docks and into the melted snow.

The Parks and Recreation Department recently added an outdoor basketball court at the Bloedel facility, and most days the court activity could be mistaken for a scene from the movie "White Men Can't Jump." It also has the lake's only public boat launch within city limits, and concession stands and watercraft rentals in-season. The pavilion building at Bloedel is host to many community events. It is a polling place, a community basketball gym and may be reserved by contacting the Bellingham Parks and Recreation office.

Written by Ken Brierly

Marine Park

Address
200 Harris Ave.
Bellingham WA, 98225

Hours
Every day Dawn - Dusk

Directions:
From 1-5 Old Fairhaven Parkway exit, go down the parkway to
12th street and go right. Turn left on Harris and follow the road
to the water and the park.

Features
Bathrooms, Picnic Area, Picnic Tables, Walking Trails

Description
Marine Park isn't a big park. It doesn't have swing sets or baseball
diamonds or tennis courts. It doesn't have jogging trails or grassy
fields. It's not in a remote area, far off the beaten path. What it
does have is a quiet stretch of land along the bay with a fantastic
view of the sound and San Juan Islands.

The narrow strip of land that comprises the park is huddled
behind the shipyards of Fairhaven. There is a covered picnic area
and a few lonely park benches strewn along the waterfront, but
is otherwise free of buildings. It is surprisingly peaceful — the
only sounds that can be heard are the drone of ships in the harbor and the calls of seabirds. The shoreline is abrupt even at low
tide, as are many of the Puget Sound's beaches — a short ridge
created out of boulders and concrete between grass and ocean.
The park is perhaps best experienced at sunrise or sunset when
the dramatic light dances on the water and the ridges of the
islands.

Although not part of the park itself, access to the railroad tracks
can be easily had near the park's entrance or by climbing the
trestle in the corner of the park. A short walk down the tracks
will bring one to a small grassy point with interesting rock forma-
tions, just parallel a ringing bell buoy. From here, the view is even
more magnificent, with views of the San Juans and waterways
just northwest of Burlington. On a clear day, the outline of the
Olympic Range is visible in the distance. The beach and train
tracks also offers an interesting vista stretching to the south
along the shore — and an invitation to walk along the water further.

Written by Glen Berry

Outdoors

Sehome Hill Arboretum

Address
Bellingham WA, 98225

Hours
Every day Dawn - Dusk

Directions:
To get to the Sehome Hill Arboretum, take I-5's Samish Way exit to Bill MacDonald Parkway. As you approach Western past Sehome High School, turn right on the access road across the street from the Washington Archive building. Parking is available at the end of the road.

Features
Walking Trails

Description
It is an island of woodland in the heart of Bellingham. Spanning 165 acres of the Sehome hilltop, the Sehome Hill Arboretum crowns the city. This vast preserve of park land offers 5.9 miles of winding trails up, down and around the hilltop. Lightly used, nature lovers may witness birds and squirrel's frolicking among the canopies of the towering evergreens. Deer are also abundant at the arboretum, as it serves as a haven from the increasingly developed surrounding area. The natural setting presents an abundance of indigenous plants, shrubs and trees.

All of Sehome Hill Arboretum's trails come to a head at the hill-top where an opposing lookout tower stands. The only structure in the park, the 80-foot tower boasts an impressive view of the city, the San Juan Islands and beyond. Walkers, joggers and bicy-clists tread the gravel trail paths. Disability access to the arbore-tum is limited due to the gravel trails, steep inclines and stairs. Consistent with its character as a semi-wild enclave, keep in mind that the park lacks restroom facilities, picnic areas and benches. Parking is available at the south entrance of the arboretum.

Visitors of the arboretum must also be aware that cougars have been sighted within the park's boundaries on occasion. If any sightings have been recently reported, Western's University Police will have warnings posted at the main access points of the area. Deer provide an ample source of food for a cougar and they don't randomly attack people, but one might pose a danger if it feels threatened. To avoid an encounter with a cougar, be sure you or your pet make some noise during your travel and stay on the main trails. Otherwise, should you encounter a cougar, don't run. Experts recommend tactics such as waving your arms wildly and throwing sticks and rocks in the cat's direction. Also, be sure to report any sightings to city or campus police.

Written by Ken Brierly

Whatcom Falls

Address
1401 Electric Ave.
Bellingham WA, 98226

Hours
Every day Dawn - Dusk

Directions:
Travel east on Lakeway Drive past Bayview Cemetery. Turn left
into the park from the stoplight at Lakeway and Silver Beach
Road. Another entrance is on Electric Avenue.

Features
Bathrooms, Picnic Area, Picnic Tables, Swimming Areas, Tennis
Courts, Walking Trails

Description
Bellingham has some great urban parks, and Whatcom Falls Park
may be its finest. A veritable 241-acre jewel, the waterfalls eternal-
ly beat in the heart of the city. From the central parking area, the
roar of the water attracts visitors to a paved path leading to a
sandstone bridge that spans Whatcom Creek. From there, the
main waterfall may be appreciated. The bridge is impressive: a
beautiful vestige of Chuckanut sandstone built in 1939 as a project of the Roosevelt-sponsored Works Progress Administration.

Areas of the park near the creek are wooded with indigenous
trees and shrubs. Past the bridge, the park's trails become dirt
and gravel paths that lead to other sections of the creek. Leashes
are not required for dogs in this section of the park. Aquatic
adventurers are familiar with a section of the park known as
"The Whirlpool," where daring swimmers leap from a 60-foot
cliff, plunging into the cold waters below. However, this is not a
supervised swimming area, so jump at your own risk.

Those who have visited the park know there is a lot more to
Whatcom Falls than just waterfalls. The eastern-most half of the
park consists of fields, tennis courts and a fish hatchery. Groups
may also reserve covered picnic areas by contacting the Parks
and Recreation office. The park has a fishing pond for kids less
than 12 years. With parental supervision, this is a great spot
to teach children the basics of angling. Take advantage of the
children's fishing derby during the opening week of trout season.

Written by Ken Brierly

Cornwall

Address
2800 Cornwall Ave.
Bellingham WA, 98225

Hours
Every day Dawn - Dusk

Directions:
From the I-5 Meridian exit, drive south on Meridian Street toward the city's center. Past the country club, two park entrances will be on the left past the Birchwood intersection.   ·

Features
Baseball Diamonds, Bathrooms, Horseshoe Pits, Picnic Area, Picnic Tables, Tennis Courts, Walking Trails

Description
Cornwall Park is not your ordinary, run-of-the-mill city park with perfect shrubbery, beauty bark and impeccably manicured lawns. It is a northwest park through and through, populated mainly by large firs, hemlocks and cedars, which block out the sun. The temperature under these trees is 10-degrees cooler than outside the park, and, true to form, the ground is covered with ferns and pine needles.

There is no road through the park, only two entrances that don't quite meet in the middle. However, they offer access to the recreational areas in the park. There are tennis courts, jogging and fitness trails, bike routes and the obligatory park benches, childrens' playground and public bathrooms. Interestingly enough, there are so many horseshoe pits lining the center of the park, a national shoeing competition could be hosted at Cornwall. The Jackson Fitness Trail is designed with a number of different stations along the route for various exercises. The jogging trails are less defined, winding over roots and rocks through the woods. There are also moss-covered benches tucked deep in the park for the less-ambitious visitor.

At both edges of the park and tucked away inside, stretches of green grass present themselves for volleyball and baseball — although summer is the only time of year dry enough for these sports. The newer part of the park now offers a wading pool and covered picnic area. Here you will also find a bridge and an area to walk along Squalicum Creek where it flows through the park.

Written by Glen Berry

Maritime Heritage Park

Address
Old Town

Hours
Every day Dawn - Dusk

Directions:
From Lakeway, take Holly Street through downtown. It is located in Old Town on the right.

Features
Picnic Area, Picnic Tables, Walking Trails, Wheelchair Accessible

Description
Commonly know as "the fish hatchery," Maritime Heritage Park is currently a work-in-progress — soon to consist of much more than a fish hatchery, a few trails, some lookout areas and the Shrimp Shack:

An ambitious project to revamp and expand a downtown park broke ground August 1998 in Old Town which will create a pedestrian corridor from Central Avenue by Prospect Street, through Maritime Heritage Park to Citizen's Dock by Georgia Pacific. A Central Avenue lookout will crown a hillside amphitheater and is currently being constructed in Maritime Heritage Park; lamplit pedestrian paths and waterfront day-use docks are expected to be added along with aesthetic enhancements as city planners, the Port of Bellingham and Old Town merchants attempt to improve the image of Old Town, making it a more desirable stop for families, shoppers and tourists. "This is exciting for us because we're just getting started," said Tara Hardesty, a city planner who has helped design and coordinate the project. "It's not very attractive now, but it will be."

The project will help enhance the historical aspects of the area, and will happen in three phases during five or six years — the first two phases will be completed within five years at a cost of approximately $5 million, Hardesty said. Most of the park improvements will be completed by 2000. The project is financed in part by the city's general fund and by a Community Development Block Grant from the Federal Government's Housing and Urban Development, Beyond Greenways, Old Town Business Association, private donations and other grants.

The only hitch of the project lies within the third phase — the day-use docks and the mouth of the Whatcom Creek waterway. In order to allow recreational boaters access to docks off Roeder Avenue, at least a portion of the mud flats below must be dredged. Deemed contaminated, a plan must be drafted by the Department of Natural Resources, City of Bellingham, Port of Bellingham, Georgia Pacific West Inc., Army Corps of Engineers and possibly the state Department of Ecology.

Outdoors

Most of these groups will also foot the bill for cleaning up cont-aminated areas within Bellingham Bay, and costs could range anywhere from $7.5 million to $85 million, according to Port of Bellingham
estimates.

Three factors figure into determining the ultimate solution for the clean-up process: First, the outermost part of the channel by G.P. is a federal channel, which will put some of the final plan's emphasis on commerce and shipping. Also, Whatcom Creek's Chinook salmon run must be considered, as the mud flats are critical to the survival of the salmon. Another factor affecting the plan is a community interest to improve public access to the city's waterfront. The waterway cleanup will not begin until 2001, and work of this magnitude usually follows a period of public-comment, decisions, and a design phase. Port environmental specialists are leaning toward a plan that will keep the cleanup relatively inexpensive while improving habitat for salmon, crab and other critters; day use access to the docks will also be possible. The challenge lies in satisfying all the competing interests.

Written by Ken Brierly

Boulevard Park

Address
South State St. and Bayview Dr.
Bellingham WA, 98225

Hours
Every day Dawn - Dusk

Directions:
Boulevard Park can be accessed by
the lower parking lot, right where
South State turns into 11th St. The
park entrance is easy to miss so look
carefully. You can also park up above
closer to Bellingham along South
State St.

Features
Picnic Tables, Bathrooms, Walking
Trails

Description
Tucked below South Hill, Boulevard Park presents the opportunity to enjoy the Bellingham Bay waterfront. However, don't expect sandy beaches and a boat launch — Boulevard Park has an abrupt, rocky shoreline that protects it from being reclaimed by the sea. This beautiful park bears little resemblance to its industrial history — if you look closely you can see pilings which were used around the turn of the century for docks, canneries and lumber mills. The park also consists of a strip along the bluff above the main park (accessible by a staircase tower) which provides a good place to watch the sunset.

Boulevard Park is an ideal place to play Frisbee because of long, wide stretches of grass. However, amateurs beware — the stray Frisbee can go into the bay. Also, the sea breeze makes the park a great place to spot kites on a windy day. From the park, you can walk on a gravel trail that will take you all the way downtown, terminating right behind the Pepper Sister's restaurant on North State Street. You can access this trail after crossing the railroad tracks under the overhead staircase. Another option is to walk the other direction toward Fairhaven on a boardwalk along the water — a popular spot for crabbing and fishing.

On a sunny day, Boulevard Park can be one of the most beautiful places in Bellingham — and one of the busiest. The parking lot usually has enough room, however, on special occasions (like the Fourth of July), try parking above along the street. Make sure to bring plenty of suntan lotion and your walking shoes.

Written by Wayne Berry

Lily and Lizard Lakes

Address
Barrel Springs Rd.
Bellingham WA, 98225

Hours
Every day Dawn - Dusk

Directions:
Get off the I-5 South at exit 240 (Alger), turn right and then take a left on Barrel Springs road. Take a right on a well-graveled road sign posted "Blanchard Mountain Trail. Park at the lower parking lot or continue another 2 miles to the upper parking lot.

Features
Biking Trails

Description
Every foot of the five mile hike up Blanchard Mountain to Lily and Lizard Lakes is well worth the effort. After parking in the lower parking lot, I began hiking from the trailhead 500 feet further down the road. The trail begins with a gentle incline and several switchbacks allowing the hiker to warm up. There is not much tree cover here, but soon I had a great view of Mt. Baker and the surrounding valley. About a mile later I arrived at the second parking lot. From there, I turned left on the gravel road and a minute later was back on the trail. This entrance is also the overnight camping registration station. The trail is well-maintained by Whatcom County's Backcountry Horsemen's Association and is thus open not only to mountain bikers and hikers, but also to horses.

Before hitting the depths of the forest, the trail borders the tree line, offering fabulous views of Skagit Valley, the San Juan Islands, and on a clear day, Mt. Rainer and the Olympic Mountains. Steeper inclines and switchbacks then take you another three miles to the top where there is a split in the trail: turn right and head a mile down the path toward Lizard Lake where there are camping and horse facilities (even rustic stabling facilities for camping with horses) or go left about 500 yards to Lily Lake. There is an additional split in the trail, giving you the choice to head straight to the Oyster Dome and the Bat Caves or turn right to Lily Lake.

Whether you like hiking or biking or horseback riding, the real reward is to sit by either lake for a while, far from the city, and to remember that silence is the natural sound of the world.

Note: there are campsites at both lakes with toilet facilities and fire pits. The elevation is approx. 1500 feet. Allow about 5 to 8 hours for the trip, bring a snack and plenty of water.

Written by Hilary Higgins

Outdoors

Connelly Creek

Address   **Hours**
Donovan Avenue at 30th Street   Every day Dawn - Dusk
Bellingham WA, 98225

Directions:
From I-5, take the Fairhaven exit. On Old Fairhaven
Parkway at turn right at 30th Street. Two blocks later, cross
Donovan Avenue and park in the gravel strip along
Donovan. You are at the South entrance of Connelly Creek
Trail.

Features
Kid Friendly, Walking Trails, Biking Trails

Description
One of the best trails in Bellingham for families with
young children is the Connelly Creek Trail, winding
through South Bellingham's Connelly Creek Nature
Corridor.

The trail can be started at Donovan and 30th Street, or at
the corner of Douglas and 30th Street, next to Joe's
Garden. A map of the path at the Donovan trail head features drawings by students of the Bellingham Cooperative
School showing some of the animals that inhabit the corridor. As you walk the trail you might discover rabbits, fox,
deer, raccoons or dragonflies.

Two things make this trail especially attractive to families
with young children: its natural diversity and its limited
elevation gain. In a short distance, children can cross a
meadow, walk through a young alder grove, enter a forest
filled with large cedars, and cross Connelly creek over foot
bridges. The trail takes walkers past swamps filled with
pungent skunk cabbage and an earthen water retention
dam that can be explored.

The trail has no real hills to climb, only the occasional
small slope. You can cover the entire trail out and back in
less than half an hour. If children find the trail too long,
one thing that never fails to revive their interest in completing the hike is a unique counting game.

Beginning at the Donovan entrance, a series of birdhouses
attached to trees along the trail starts in the alder grove
and stretches the remaining length of trail. The hike goes
faster when everyone tries to be the first to find the next
birdhouse along the path. Over the years, this game has
transformed whining, foot-dragging children into excited
and laughing explorers. This game has become so much a

part of the hike that now my children usually initiate it when we walk the trail.

Because the trail is so close, it has become a part of the daily routine for many hikers. Walking it on a daily basis, its easy to feel close to nature, watching plants sprouting in the spring, blackberries ripening in autumn, and snow sifting down through tree branches on a crisp cold winter afternoon.

Written by Rob Olason

Outdoors

Fragrance and Lost Lakes

Address
Chuckanut Drive
Bellingham WA, 98225

Directions:
On Chuckanut Drive (State Highway 11) 7 miles south of
Bellingham across from the entrance to Larrabee State Park

Description
Fragrance Lake, by its very name, would beckon any hiker. Access
is from either the Clayton Beach parking lot or the Fragrance
Lake Trailhead on Chuckanut drive. The Clayton Beach lot affords
ample parking with accessible restrooms but puts the hiker on a
graveled logging road for a substantial distance. The preferred origin is the Fragrance Lake Trailhead across from the entrance to
Larrabee State Park. There, the hiker is immediately enfolded in
the ferned and forested coolness of the timberland. Lost Lake is
best accessed from its trailhead at a spur off the Fragrance Lake
trail. It'll be a 3 mile trek from that point to Lost Lake, making the
in and out mileage for your journey an ambitious 10 miles.

At the Fragrance Lake trailhead on Chuckanut, the path quickly
bisects the interurban trail so proceed directly across it. Wooded
gates at intervals make this a "Hikers Only, No Bicycles" hike. It's
a 1.8 mile hike up to the lake through shaded forest. "Up" is an
aptly chosen directive. Some would say "steep" but it's more of a
steady-drumbeat-of-an-ascent to the 1100' elevation. Early in the
hike you'll be presented with a side route option to an overlook.
Take it. It's a short, flat passage and your pulse and respiratory
rate can come back to normal. And, you'll be treated to a gasp of
a perfectly composed Puget Sound panorama.

Go right at the fork when a peek of Fragrance Lake is in sight.
You'll come upon hand hewn benches and a small flattening of
land that offers prime viewing of the clean, clear lake and textured woodlands surrounding it. It's perfect for the lunch you
just earned or the nap you deserve. While enjoying the striking
beauty, interrupt your repose long enough to contemplate the
stiff case Fragrance Lake makes against the notion, "the joy is the
journey".

Written by Debra Exley

Interurban Trail

Address
c. 1800 Old Fairhaven Pkway
Bellingham WA, 98225

Directions:
You can either pick up the trail at
Fairhaven Park or at the official
Trailhead off of Old Fairhaven
Pkway about 1/2 mile to the east of
Fairhaven proper.

Features
Walking Trails

Description
It's not difficult to see why the
Interurban Trail is one of the most popular trails in Bellingham.
The variance in foliage, ecosystems, views and branching side
trails have much to offer the day hiker or biker. The trailhead
begins at Old Fairhaven Parkway (or Fairhaven Park) on the south
side of town and snakes through the woods along the western
slope of Chuckanut Mountain for roughly six miles.

The trail is well groomed and flat — the remains of an old rail
transit system with fine crushed gravel that can accommodate
several hikers walking abreast. The Interurban then breaks out on
Old Samish Road, which connects Lake Samish with Chuckanut
Drive. On the other side of the road is Arroyo Park. You can then
pick up the trail again a short distance away on California Street.
This part of the trail continues on the side of the mountain above
Chuckanut Drive for another 4 miles to Larrabee State Park. From
here, there are also intersections with the North Chuckanut
Mountain Trail, the Teddy Bear Cove Trail and the Fragrance and
Lost lakes trail.

The beauty of the trail can be easily seen in the environment it
crosses. The first mile of the trail winds through wetlands filled
with birds and flowering plants springing out of the brackish
water. The next section of trail transitions into the cool canopy of
evergreens, the forest floor populated with scattered sword ferns.
As the hiker continues on towards the trail's terminus at
Larrabee, occasional breaks in the trees offer a view of Puget
Sound. The spectacular vistas of the San Juan Islands is perhaps
the highest recommendation for the Interurban Trail — a must
see on a summer sunset.

Written by Glen Berry

Pine and Cedar Lakes

Address
36th Street
Bellingham WA, 98225

Hours
Every day Dawn - Dusk

Directions:
From Old Fairhaven, drive out 12th Street to Chuckanut Drive. About half a mile past Fairhaven Park, turn left on Old Samish. Drive for a couple miles and watch out for the Pine and Cedar Lakes turnoff and trail head on the south side of the road. The lakes are a few miles up the hill.

Features
Walking Trails

Description
If you plan on hiking to these mountain lakes, follow these five instructions for maximum enjoyment:

(No. 1) Unless you begin training a couple weeks before you go, don't attempt a hike to Pine and Cedar Lakes with a case of canned beverages in your backpack. Why? Because apparently this Whatcom County Parks trail was created before the advent of switchbacks -- it's straight uphill, no mercy. So whether you plan to day hike or stay overnight, pack lightly and use a framed backpack that provides optimum support — otherwise, this 2.5 mile hike wile seem like 25 miles.

(No. 2) If you enjoy trout fishing, bring your pole. If you don't you will begin suffering at around 6 p.m. any evening during fishing season: The bugs begin dancing just above the surface of the lakes' placid waters. Then a flurry of fish begin jumping and feasting like a pack of mad flesh-eating piranhas -- only they're not piranhas, they are brown and rainbow trout. There are so many trout in these lakes that if you can't catch one by conventional means, you might want to try flailing about in the water with a large stick. As a last resort, leaning over the water and batting at the fish with your hand while growling ferociously has proven to be successful.

(No. 3) Bring lots of fishing tackle, cause you'll lose some. You must understand that fishing Pine or Cedar is nothing like fishing Lake Padden. First of all, only a few trails provide limited access to the lakes' banks, and near these few access points, the surrounding shrubbery makes casting your line a treacherous affair. Also, the lakes are full of snags – fallen trees from years and decades past become aquatic jungle gyms for fish and microorganisms. The fallen trees will also pirate your new silver-spinning lure that you just paid 3 bucks for earlier in the day. So bring plenty of tackle.

(**No. 4**) Bring bug repellent, drinking water, a trash bag and bug repellent. This is a wild place, so plan ahead and make a list. When you get there, don't worry: those are only mosquitoes, not massive, mutated hummingbirds.

(**No. 5**) If no burn ban is in effect, bring firewood. Everyone knows that it's not wise to burn wood found on the forest floor, but even if you wanted to, there's no wood there anyway. The forest that envelopes Pine and Cedar at the top of Chuckanut Mountain is a canopy of massive evergreens towering above a few sword ferns and an occasional salmonberry bush — no dry and shrubby tinder anywhere. If a fire is not important to your camping experience, at least pack a little gas stove so you can fry up those tasty fishies that required $30 of tackle for you to reel in.

Written by Ken Brierly

Blanchard Mountain

Address
Barrel Springs Rd.
Bellingham WA, 98225

Hours
Every day Dawn - Dusk

Directions:
To get to the Blanchard Mountain trailhead, take I-5 exit 240 and head west on Lake Samish Rd. Turn left on Barrel Springs Road then right after a mile onto a gravel road marked with a "Blanchard Mountain Trail" sign.

Features
Biking Trails

Description
Blanchard Mountain is not a ride for the faint-of-heart or the out-of-shape, unless you're a little crazy and stupid — like myself. This ride might be a little better as a day hike instead of a ride — unless you're an absolute stud, you'll be pushing your bike at least half of the way up the mountain.

The entire trail is single track, up hill, with plenty of rocks and roots. If you're able to persevere through the climb, the rewards at the end are well worth the hard work. At the very top of the mountain is the Oyster Dome amphitheater, a 200-foot cliff above the Bat Caves with a sweeping view of Chuckanut Bay, Skagit Valley and the San Juan Islands. A campsite is available at the Oyster Dome or at Lily Lake if you want to spend a lot of time up here. If not, I would recommend at least three hours for this ride — you'll want to take some time to take in the view.

To get to the Blanchard Mountain trailhead, take I-5 exit 240 and head west. Turn left on Barrel Springs Road then right after a mile onto a gravel road marked with a "Blanchard Mountain Trail" sign. Follow the gravel road past the first parking area and the first sign for the trail, staying to the right at the fork. You will see the trail registration station at the trailhead on the left side of the road. Park off to the right in the lot past the trailhead. Follow the trail for about three miles, staying to the right at the first two turns. When you get to the sign for Lily and Lizard lakes, follow the sign to the left to Lily Lake. Once you get to the Lily Lake turnoff (1,000 meters past the sign), you can turn right to go to the lake or continue straight to the Oyster Dome. Take the next right turn, it will be marked as "ROCK oyster dome." You're almost there. Follow the trail the rest of the way up to the most spectacular views in the area.

Written by Jason Rose

Lake Padden

Address
Samish Way
Bellingham WA, 98225

Hours
Every day Dawn - Dusk

Directions:
To get to the trails, take I-5 exit 252 in Bellingham, then turn southeast on Samish Way and head up the hill. Lake Padden is a couple miles ahead on your right.

Features
Biking Trails

Description
This is my favorite area to mountain bike in Bellingham — there's a little bit for everyone here. To get to the trails, take I-5 exit 252 in Bellingham, then turn southeast on Samish Way and head up the hill. Lake Padden is a couple miles ahead on your right.

A gentle 2.6-mile loop suitable for riders of all ages and skill levels runs around the lake. For the more daring, plenty of mud, logs, roots and switchbacks can be found on the trails to the east. From the sign at the southeast end of the park, turn to your left and follow the trail for about a mile until you reach the power lines. Go straight under the power lines and follow the trail through the woods. The trail will come to a "T" after a quarter mile. For the really daring, take the next left and follow the trail around, staying right on the turns. You'll be challenged by some hardcore grades with some fun switchbacks. After about four or five switchbacks, take a left turn and follow the trail up the next hill, where you'll find more good drop-offs and tight turns. This trail will eventually take you back to the parking lot.

Watch out — the second part of this ride is one of the few places that I've done and end-O. If you don't take the left turn, you will eventually end up on the trail that you came in on. For the intermediate rider, continue straight past the turnoff to the more advanced track. You will be going up the same stretch the advanced rider would be coming down on. Stay to the left on all the turns and follow the trail around. Both trails loop around to where you started.

Written by Jason Rose

Pine and Cedar Bike Trail

Address
36th Street
Bellingham WA, 98225

Hours
Every day Dawn - Dusk

Directions:
From Old Fairhaven, drive out 12th Street to Chuckanut Drive. About half a mile past Fairhaven Park, turn left on Old Samish. Drive for a couple miles and watch out for the Pine and Cedar Lakes turnoff and trail head on the south side of the road. The lakes are a few miles up the hill.

Features
Walking Trails, Biking Trails

Description
The trails to Pine and Cedar Lakes make for a strenuous ride, but at least most of the uphill stretches are on logging roads. This also means that you can just fly on the way back down the hill without worrying about big roots and rocks on the path. Unfortunately, if you're among the riders that can't stomach the fumes of skunk cabbage, this is not the ride for you. Though you can't get away from the stuff up here, other than that, the ride is beautiful.

To get to the trailhead take I-5 exit 250 and go west on the Old Fairhaven Parkway until you see the Interurban Trail parking area on your left side. Go left onto the Interurban Trail and follow it across Old Samish Road and into Arroyo Park. At the top of the hill in Arroyo, turn left onto the Lost Lake trail. This will lead you up a steep climb the average rider probably can't bike. At the top of the hill you will find a nice, wide logging road leading further into the hills. After following this road for a little while the Lost Lake road will turn to the right up the hill. Continue on straight. You will follow this road for quite a distance, going uphill most of the way. Eventually, the road will become a single track — you're about half way there. Continue until you reach the Cedar and Pine Lakes hiking trail. Take a right on the trail — you're almost there. After about half a mile, you will see the turnoff for Cedar Lake.

Riding another quarter mile or so will get you to the Pine Lakes trail. There's no good riding around the lakes, so leave your bike up top and enjoy the lakes on foot. I would suggest allowing 4 to 5 hours to do this ride if you want to take some time to enjoy the lakes. Both lakes have multiple campsites with fire pits should you want to extend the trip.

Written by Jason Rose

Galbraith Mountain

Address
Galbraith Lane
Bellingham WA, 98225

Hours
Every day Dawn - Dusk

Outdoors

Directions:
To get to Galbraith Mountain follow the directions to Lake Padden.
Continue past Lake Padden on Samish Way until you find Galbraith
Lane. Park in the lot across the street to the right.

Features
Biking Trails

Description
Galbraith is for intermediate and expert riders. Miles of logging trails
weave throughout the mountain. Be considerate and obey private
property signs and, as always, be sure to wear a helmet. To get to
Galbraith Mountain, follow the directions to Lake Padden. Continue
past Padden on Samish Way until you reach Galbraith Lane.

Ride up Galbraith lane. Turn right when the private road starts and
continue through the gate. Now it's up to you — there are just too
many trails through here. If you keep riding up the hill you will
eventually come to the radio towers. If you're into speed, turn around
here and you can take a 1,000-foot descent down the road that you
just came up. If you are into a more technical trail, continue past the
towers on the trail that leads off to the left. It will eventually meet
the road that you came up. It has a couple of brutal drop-offs and the
ruts are getting pretty bad with all the motor cross riders, but it the
best single stretch of trail that I've found so far.

Anywhere you go on the mountain is great. There's more terrain out
there than you could handle in a day and it's all fun with ramps up
almost every log and a couple good streams to cross. Be sure to hit it
after it rains — the entire mountain turns into an old fashioned
Pacific Northwest mud bowl. Starting from the north side of the
mountain offers a more difficult ascent but the hard work going up
makes for more fun coming down.

Access Galbraith from the other side. Take I-5 exit 253 and turn east
on Lakeway Drive. When you get past the cemetery, turn left into
Whatcom Falls Park and park you car. From here, ride back the way
you came across Lakeway Drive at the light. Follow Kenoyer Drive
until you come to Alvarado. Turn left on Alvarado and follow it until
you come to a gate at a logging road. From here, just follow the logging road up the mountain. If you want the most speed and air with
the smallest effort just ride up until the road comes to a "T" at the left
and turn around. If you're more adventurous take the "T" to the left
and follow the road up the hill. After a little while the road will start
to go back downhill. Off to the right will be some single tracks —
pick one and follow it. It's hard to go wrong, just explore from there.
If anyone out there know the names of the different trail systems on
Galbraith and Lookout mountains, I'd appreciate it if you would give
me an e-mail and let me know.

Written by Jason Rose

Mt. Baker Ski Area

Address
It's on top of the mountain.
Bellingham WA, 98225

Directions: Go up to Sunset Drive and head east for an hour and fifteen minutes. Stop when you can't drive anymore. It's kind of hard to miss.

Description
Mount Baker is the most defining feature of Whatcom County. This mountain towers over the area at nearly 11,000 feet in elevation and is the second-most active volcano in the Cascade Range, after St. Helens. When the wind blows just right and the skies are clear, a plume of steam occasionally rises from Sherman Crater, Baker's active caldera.

Forty miles east of Bellingham, the Mt. Baker Ski Area registers more annual snowfall than any other ski area in North America. It is commonly referred to as the "birthplace of snowboarding" and, appropriately, is host to the world's premier snowboarding competition, the Annual Legendary Banked Slalom. Located in the Mount Baker/Snoqualmie National Park, overnight lodging facilities are not possible, however, the White Salmon Day Lodge serves skiers as a serene rest area. Skiers and boarders can order a beer at the lodge, have lunch, then hit the slopes again, rejuvenated. The lodge is only a couple years old; of other lodges that pre-existed it, the first one may have been the most famous — it was the location for the movie classic "White Christmas," but burned down soon after filming.

During ski season — usually starting sometime in November until the end of March — eight lifts transport skiers to runs every day from 9 a.m. to 4 p.m. Monday through Wednesday, adult passes cost $18.50; Thursday and Friday, $20; and $30 on weekends and holidays. For those who have skied at other places in North America, notice that passes are among the cheapest in the country. Also, the powder is second-to-none.

Written by Ken Brierly

Film & Art

To describe the arts scene in Bellingham as "avid," "vibrant" or "diverse" wouldn't necessarily be incorrect, although grossly understated. The city is literally teeming with poets, writers and artists of all sorts. Binding them together are the myriad of support organizations, non-profit groups and galleries which showcase the artists' work.

Rich in art from every medium, Whatcom County boasts a bevy of displays within its galleries. Gallery showings are continuous at many locations, including at the respected Whatcom Museum of History and Art, and campus locations at Western Washington University.

Art is literally everywhere you look, from the collection of outdoor sculptures spread across the city, to art galleries found every few blocks downtown. Organizers take advantage of this concentration of galleries to sponsor regular "gallery walks," guiding crowds from venue to venue.

This is not to mention a rapidly growing film scene. Independent video shops are now joined by the Pickford Cinema - Bellingham's only independent movie theater. Summertime affords residents the opportunity to take part in an outdoor cinema as well - an event popular with people of all ages.

Whatcom County also has a proud sense of its frontier history, preserved by museums with permanent displays, special showings and historical tours in the form of guided walks and even cruises on Bellingham Bay.

With ever-changing national exhibits complementing locally rooted displays, the community's museums offer a compelling glimpse into the past.

Film & Art

Bellis Fair Cinemas

Address
Bellis Fair Parkway
Bellingham WA, 98226

Directions
Head north on the guide past the Country Club and freeway
overpass. Turn left at the intersection with Red Robin and
McDonald's. The theaters are just inside the mall's main entrance.

Features
Smoke-free

Description
When most people think of movie stars and celebrities,
Hollywood comes to mind. Inside Bellis Fair mall, there lies a
microcosm of Tinseltown where film watchers may take in as
much glitter and stardom as necessary. Bellis Fair Cinemas is the
largest movie house in town, playing all the biggest blockbusters
starring our favorite celebs. The six large screens, clean surroundings, and real butter on an endless supply of popcorn make Bellis
Fair Cinemas a refreshing getaway from the monotony of not
being famous.

One struggles to think of a better way to rest the feet after a
treacherous day of battle amongst a mob of mall shoppers. Its
proximity to restaurants and other businesses at the mall makes
it a viable destination for a date, especially that awkward first
date when conversation might be sparse. The red carpet spanning the cinema's lobby guides movie viewers past a counter —
packed with a massive assortment of candy and popcorn — with
soda fountains perched on top. For those who arrive early, pass
the time by playing a variety of popular arcade games in the
lobby. Inside the large air-conditioned theaters, the seats are not
too confining, and are even somewhat comfortable. When decid-
ing how to best occupy free time, consider dodging the season's
harsher elements by catching a flick at Bellis Fair.

Once through the doors of the theater, the movie buzz starts to
pump through one's veins in anticipation of the mega-hit about
to be witnessed. Moviegoers quell with excitement as the theater's lights dim and the curtain slowly rises, unveiling the "silver
screen." Like any other theater complex in the nation, scores of
movie previews give consumers a sneak peak of the studios' latest productions soon to visit Bellis Fair Cinemas. Due to skyrock-
eting movie production costs, box office prices continue to esca-
late at a rate of something like 1,000 times the rate of inflation;
though this figure is completely fabricated, make it an incentive
for attending movies on Mondays, as ticket prices are reduced
that day. Also, keep an eye out for matinee discounts.

Written by Tyler Watson

Sunset Cinemas

Address
1135 E. Sunset Dr.
Bellingham WA, 98226

Directions: Take the Sunset exit off of I-5. It's tucked off in the freeway (west) end of the Sunset Square shopping mall. It's hard to find, because the entrance is tucked back in a little alley.

Features
Bathrooms, Smoke-free, Wheelchair Accessible

Description
The big name theaters in Bellingham are all part of one big happy family. Bellis Fair Cinema, Sehome Cinema 3 and Sunset Square Cinema 6 are all owned by Regal Cinemas. Bellis Fair is the Papa Bear in this Goldilocks tale, Sehome is Baby Bear, and Sunset Square gets to play Middle Mama. The latter doesn't show the biggest blockbusters like Bellis, nor do they show the limited release and artsy stuff that Sehome picks up. Sunset Square tends to find the happy medium between the two.

Sunset Square is a very nice theater. It's got a modern feel, with lots of cool blue neon and very high ceilings, ample concessions with the traditional $3 drink. The theater can be very popular, especially on children's matinees and opening nights. Arriving early and buying tickets is recommended, especially since it allows time to make a short trip to the nearby grocery store for some M&Ms to sneak in.

They've got six screens, two big ones, two medium sized, and two little guys for the shows that just refuse to die. The larger theaters have DTS stereo sound. Mondays are "Cheap Movie Night" (that's what all my friends call it anyway), excluding "star" attractions. All shows before 6 p.m. are also cheaper matinees. I've actually caught a fair number of flicks at Sunset, and I've never been disappointed by the place. The seats are always comfortable, the popcorn always fresh and the floor always kept clear of stray Ju-Ju-Bees. While it's no Mann's Chinese Theater, at least you won't find any nasty surprises either.

Written by Dave Shepherd

Film & Art

Sehome Cinema 3

Address
3330 Fielding Avenue
Bellingham WA, 98225

Directions:
Just South of Sehome Village (with the big Haggen's), right next door to the Keg.

Features
Wheelchair Accessible

Description
Since Fall 1998, Sehome Cinema 3 has been known as Regal Cinemas, which bought out Act III theaters. It hasn't seemed to change the nature of this theater much. This theater doesn't carry the mega-hit blockbusters. With three screens and a relatively out-of-the-way location, it caters to a different audience than the Bellis Fair and Sunset Square cinemas. Some, including myself, would argue that this is a good thing.

Even before the change of ownership, Sehome/Regal Cinemas was featuring the more intellectual films coming out of Hollywood. With three screens, the venue's forced selectivity generally yields a higher "decent-entertainment-to-garbage ratio." Big-ticket foreign films, artsy flicks, and indie films that can't afford a multi-million dollar media blitz— they all seem to find their way onto Sehome's screens. I will admit, I even look forward to the annual arrival of Spike and Mike's Festival of Sick and Twisted Animation, so it's not just Shakespeare that sets this place apart from its big-budget partners down the road.

Beyond the playbill, the theater is pretty typical— enthusiastic employees in silly vests, lots of burgundy decor and popcorn at only 25 cents a kernel! The screens are medium size, featuring DTS stereo sound and about 200 seats per theater. Monday is "cheap movie night" (in the Western Washington University vernacular).

Written by Dave Shepherd

Mount Baker Theatre

Address
104 N. Commercial St.
Bellingham WA, 98225

Directions:
From Lakeway, drive down Holly
Street to Commercial and turn right.
The theater is a couple blocks down
on the right

Description
The Mount Baker Theatre is a visual
and historic landmark of downtown
Bellingham. The theater opened in
1927 as a part of the 20th Century
Fox chain — another example of
the architecturally-exotic movie
palace phenomenon of that era.
Renovated in 1995, the theater is a
plush, opulent and well cared-for
reminder of the roaring 20's.

Unlike many other Egyptian theaters from the same time period,
the Mount Baker Theatre is styled after the architecture of
Moorish Spain. It is interesting to note that all of the wood in the
lobby ceilings and the ornate columns is faux — plaster painted
to appear wooden or alabaster. Restoration was pain staking, and
contractors were brought in from outside the area to do the
time-consuming work. Complex and intricately-painted designs in
dark reds and tans cover the walls, ceilings and arches. The entire
theater has a formal and distinguished feel, including dark, wood-
en chairs that are more like small thrones, and carpets embla-
zoned with royal red lions.

The Mount Baker Theatre serves as a venue for a wide variety of
events — true to its vaudeville beginnings. Concerts of most
types, from blues, symphony and soft rock, as well as a capela
and local folk artists. The theater also hosts dance companies, theater, laser light shows and comedians, not to mention both 35mm
and 70mm films.

Written by Glen Berry

Film & Art

Pickford Cinema

Address
1416 Cornwall Avenue
Bellingham WA, 98225

Directions:
Be careful, this one is easy to miss. Go up Cornwall from the Rite-Aid and look for the white lights ringing the window of the cinema, about half-way up on the right side of the street.

Description
The Pickford Cinema is indeed a welcome addition to downtown Bellingham. As the only independent theater in Whatcom County, it fills a void by providing local filmgoers an opportunity to see films that normally pass Bellingham by. Primarily a venue for independent, foreign and underground releases, the cinema offers a film experience quite different from the more familiar multiplex theaters.

The fact that real butter is served on the popcorn says a lot. The theater doesn't boast DTTS, AC-3, THX or any other marketing gimmicks. It doesn't have a 60-foot-tall screen housed in a gigantic cavern. This is a much friendlier, intimate setting where one can actually see the faces of the people you're watching the movie with. When you watch a film at the Pickford, it's more like attending a film festival. In a smaller venue, you're closer to the screen, you're drawn into the film and you experience it along with the rest of the audience. The audience also tends to be more appreciative and involved in what is happening onscreen. This is the way film watching was intended to be. The films are more engaging, the audience more sophisticated and the overall experience is more enjoyable.

Despite its recent opening, the theater has already enjoyed a warm public response having sold out several shows to date. The history of the Pickford is short at this point, having only been open since October, 1998. It is a revival of the defunct Grand Cinema by the newly formed non-profit organization, Whatcom Film Association, which also hosts the Fairhaven Outdoor Cinema and occasional showings at the Mount Baker Theater. Another unique aspect is that the theater staff is comprised mostly of volunteers — three part-time employees operating the projection equipment, concessions, ticket taking and other aspects of the theater.

Written by Glen Berry

Outdoor Sculptures

Address

Bellingham WA, 98225

Hours
Open 24 Hours

Directions:
Simply head up to the university from downtown Bellingham or Fairhaven or, from out of town, from the MacDonald Parkway's exit. The best place to start your hunt is from WWU's Red Square. Or get an info brochure from the West Gallery Building.

Features
Kid Friendly

Description
After hearing about the outdoor sculptures on WWU's campus, a neat row of classical Greek statues came immediately to my mind. As an art enthusiast, I felt it my duty to seek them out.

During my stroll around the campus, I walked past a large stone carving that looked like a man and an animal merged together. "Interesting," I mused. But where are those outdoor sculptures?

I asked several students for directions, but to no avail. I sat down on a bench in the university's red square and stared at a huge black metallic cube balanced on its tiptoe. For something so large it was amazingly unobtrusive. I then saw a wooden totem pole-like figurine camouflaged against a red brick wall background. As I looked around the university square more closely, I set my eyes on an upright cylindrical sculpture made of hay bales. "Tasteful," I thought. Finally, I realized that I had been walking amongst the sculptures the entire time.

A good picture deserves a good frame and the red bricks of the campus provide the perfect surrounding for each piece. At first glance the sculptures appear to be placed randomly around the campus. Later I became aware of the subtle positioning of each sculpture. Whether in a shady groves of trees or in mid-square, each piece reflected its backdrop.

The very first sculpture was installed in 1960. It was commissioned from one of the Northwest's most influential artists, James Fitzgerald. Since then, Western has continued to commission pieces from major international, national, and regional artists who have addressed various themes such as the interrelationship between nature and culture, types of narration, and personal perception. An additional 22 pieces have been added since then. More pieces are in progress.

Each piece is unique, contemplative, and inspirational, just as art, not to mention a university, should be. The real fun of the outdoor sculptures is hunting for them. So why not head up there, bring the kids, and go on a sculpture safari.

Film & Art

Outdoor Sculptures (continued)

Note: Although the main concentration of sculptures is on Western's campus, the city of Bellingham has also commissioned several sculptures which are spread throughout town. Check out the corner of Magnolia and Railroad St. or on State St. next to the upper entrance of Boulevard Park.

Written by Hilary Higgins

Good Earth Pottery

Address
1000 Harris
Bellingham WA, 98225

Hours
Tues-Sat 11:00am - 6:00pm

Directions:
From the downtown area, get on State Street heading south.
Follow it around as it turns into 11th street and you will arrive in
Fairhaven. Turn right on Harris. Good Earth will be on the right at
the intersection of Harris and 10th.

Description
Good Earth Pottery is a small gallery that embraces the visitor with
layers of color, shape and a chorus of creative voices. I'm not refer-
ring to literal music but rather the wide range of originality, talent,
experience and artistic inspiration found in the hundreds of pieces
offered at Good Earth. Located in historic Fairhaven, the gallery
showcases the work of approximately 15 or so Whatcom County
artists - in fact, this makes the gallery unique. The gallery's offerings
are exclusively Whatcom County produced, which makes it an
excellent place to find items truly representative of our local talent. Good Earth Pottery products are of a wide variety and include
serving bowls, platters, mugs, goblets, soap dishes and dispensers,
candleholders, decorative tiles, planters, wall ornaments, as well as
truly distinctive objets d'art.

The gallery has been part of Fairhaven, and located in the same
building on the corner of Harris and 10th, for thirty years. The
main floor is fairly open, with a showroom at the front and a studio for potters at the rear, which is visible to visitors. Behind the
building is a small shed housing the gas-fired kiln. Not knowing
very much about the pottery process, I found it fascinating to learn
that the kiln can reach temperatures as high as 2300∞ F. The potter
can control the appearance of the finished product by manipulat-
ing the amount of oxygen and/or smoke in the kiln during the firing process. By cutting off the oxygen supply during firing, the fire
is forced to actually draw oxygen out of the clay itself. This
process, called high temperature reduction, results in a dramatic
intensity of color in the finished product. The gallery has many
beautiful examples of this technique.

In this world of endless mass marketing, national warehouse chains
and one-size-fits-all conveyor-belt production, the hand-made offerings of Good Earth Pottery are unique treasures, at prices well
worth the work and artistic fire that went into their creation.

Written by Tanya Perkins

Film & Art

Lucia Douglas Gallery

Address
1415 13th
Bellingham WA, 98225

Hours
Wed-Sat Noon - 6:00pm
Sun Noon - 6:00pm

Directions:
Corner of 13th & Larrabee in Fairhaven

Features
Kid Friendly

Description
Douglas Chapman opened the Lucia Douglas Gallery in Fairhaven in 1993. He bought an older home in town; remodeling it to house a modern gallery and show various local and regional artists' work. The Gallery is opened for exhibits ten months out of the year, with the usual exceptions being January and August.

The 2-story, modern building at the main entrance is awing. The polished cement floored main gallery is lit by track lighting suspended from a high open beam ceiling. Its industrial ambiance is in stark contrast to the work shown at eye level throughout the white environment. Billie Holiday croons as one wanders through enjoying the current show; while outdoors there is a sculpture garden used for both show and as a warm weather reception area. Questions are answered with a smile, and it takes a lot of looking to uncover the original home that served as the starting place for the gallery. Upstairs there is a commercial frame shop and downstairs is a private print studio. There is an abundance of free parking outside.

The last Sunday of the month the gallery features The Jazz Project playing in the main gallery. There is a modest charge at the door, or memberships are available. Nice to know you can enjoy local art, and listen to some good music in a clean, well lighted, pleasant space so close to home.

Written by Shelagh Considine

Tore Ofteness

Address
1417 Railroad Ave
Bellingham WA, 98225

Hours
Tues-Fri 11:00am - 5:00pm
Sat 11:00am - 4:00pm

Directions:
From Champion St, turn left on Railroad. Gallery is on your right.

Description
The snug gallery and studio of Tore Ofteness Photography reflect the talent of a free-spirited, unique individual. Since 1993, the business has been located downtown on Railroad Ave. in the Montgomery Fuel Building, built in 1936. Enter the building into the narrow gallery and your ears are soothed by soft classical music coming from the radio. A desk and two chairs in front of the gallery's back wall define a makeshift office. A cornucopia of framed color photographs line the otherwise unadorned white walls; among them is an array of atmospheric shots displaying Ofteness' deft aerial photography. One, an Ofteness icon, is an incredible shot taken 6,000 feet above Lummi Island, revealing a breathtaking panorama of Bellingham Bay, the city, and Mount Baker. Sweeping vistas of the San Juans, Mt. Shuksan, and Sehome Hill—veiled with a downy-soft cloud cover—round out the aerial display nicely.

Ofteness' candid photography renders an intrinsic ability to capture his personal vision of the world through the camera lens. Unlike typical photographers, he favors home or outdoor environments over studio settings to shoot family and wedding portraits. Instead of the traditional family and wedding mug shots, he uses a photojournalist style to capture intimate moments. He specializes in business portraits and industrial photography and serves his clients well, keeping them happy by going the extra mile.

Proceeding through a narrow doorway from the gallery into the studio brings you to where personal and business portraits are shot. A striking collection of black and white photos developed by Ofteness line the walls. Aside from a compelling shot of Seattle's Pike Place Market, most were taken during trips abroad to the Czech Republic, Vienna, Norway, London, and Mexico. Midway along the studio's left wall is a mysterious looking revolving black door that leads to the dark room. In red letters at the top of the door is written, "Beam me up, Scottie!"

Written by Nancy Steele

Film & Art

Pacific Marine

Address
700 W. Holly St.
Bellingham WA, 98225

Hours
Tues-Sat 10:00am - 6:00pm
Sun 11:00am - 5:00pm

Directions:
From Lakeway, take Holly Street through Old Town. It's on the corner of Holly and C Street.

Description
The Pacific Northwest provides a perfect backdrop to inspire area artists, helping their creativity thrive. A veritable treasure chest of local art, Pacific Marine Gallery's consignment pieces primarily conveys a nautical theme, as well as traditional Northwest Coast Native American art. Since the gallery opened in Old Town about four-years-ago, it has established itself as the place to go for those on the hunt for creations with our region's unique signature.

A stunning example of an incredible piece of coastal Indian art is the tribal depiction of an Orca head carved out of a huge vertebrae of an actual killer whale. Not only is the bone impeccably crafted, but also the irony of the carving is profound. Other symbolic coastal Indian icons are chiseled out of flat chunks of stone and are coated in a glossy finish. Basalt sculptures of the same influence are some of the more interesting works.

Also compelling is the series of colored pencil drawings showing marine perspectives of the Bellingham area before the turn-of-the-century. Incredibly detailed, these scenes draw attention because of the detail that the color shows, in contrast to the dark appearance historic photographs cast. Pacific Marine Gallery also has oil and watercolor paintings, as well as photo prints of some of this area's most scenic places ñ with a maritime theme, of course. Prices for these works range anywhere from $10 to several hundred dollars.

Written by Ken Brierly

Viking Union Gallery

Address
Viking Addition 650
Bellingham WA, 98225

Hours
Mon-Fri 10:00am - 4:00pm
Sat - 4:00pm

Directions:
Drive on Garden Street toward WWU from downtown. A half-a-block past Oak Street turn left into the metered parking lot below the Viking Union. Two-hour parking is available here. Take the elevator to the V.U.'s sixth floor. The gallery is out the elevator doors on the right. Don't let your parking meter run out; ticket prices are astronomical.

Features
Wheelchair Accessible

Description
It is rare to come across an art gallery that is showing art for art's sake, and has no interest in making money off its display. This is the purpose of the Viking Union Gallery at Western Washington University. The V.U. Gallery is a student-curated gallery sponsored by Western's student body; admission is free. The gallery serves two primary functions:

One function of the V.U. Gallery is to provide exposure for contemporary northwest artists and their works to the Western community and the residents of Bellingham. The gallery is also a venue for student and faculty artists and artists from within the community and surrounding areas. It provides a professional setting for them to exhibit their work. The exhibits vary, usually changing a few times throughout an academic quarter.

Various styles of exhibits have been known to grace the V.U. Gallery, including print, paint, sculpture and mixed-media displays. The work of children has also been showcased within the walls of the gallery. The gallery is definitely a no-frills operation, consisting simply of four walls in a single, large room.

Make it a family outing or a date. Stroll through Western's campus and check out some of its collection of award-winning outdoor sculpture. Remember: The gallery is closed Sundays and any other time school is not in session.

Written by Ken Brierly

Film & Art

Allied Arts

Address
1418 Cornwall Ave
Bellingham WA, 98225

Directions:
It's on Cornwall right up the street from the Rite Aid Store—they share some space with the Pickford Cinema.

Description
Allied Arts is an active non-profit organization whose mission statement states it is "fully committed to supporting the arts and artists of Whatcom County by fostering and creating an environment in which the arts are an integral part of the community." Allied Arts does not have a specialized focus or niche — it is dedicated to nurturing all artistic endeavors. Operating out of downtown Bellingham, Allied Arts consists of a gallery (1,100 square feet), an assembly space (1,400 square feet) with a stage and offices. The assembly space, popular with other non-profit and community groups, is available to rent for business meetings, receptions and other functions.

Allied Arts takes a holistic approach with a three-pronged strategy to supporting the arts in this region: education, festivals and exhibitions. It provides hands-on art education to area school and community groups through the Artist in the Community program — an effort to increase awareness of art at an early age. In the community itself, the organization hosts the annual "Holiday Festival of the Arts", which features artists, craftspeople and performing artists. In addition, Allied Arts assists theater productions, music and dance for local organizations. It also offers workshops focusing on creating art — from metal work to paintings — taught by local artists.

Perhaps the most important function of any arts organization is providing a means for artists to display their work. Allied Arts cooperates with other local organizations in sponsoring the Northwest International Art Competition, Chalk Art Festival and quarterly gallery walks. The organization updates its members on coming gallery events, showings and related news through their Web site and newsletter.

Written by Glen Berry

Mindport Exhibits

Address
111 Grand Ave.
Bellingham WA, 98225

Hours
Wed-Sat 10:00am - 5:00pm
Sun 10:00am - 5:00pm

Directions:
From Lakeway, take Holly Street to
Bay Street and turn right. Go right
on Magnolia and left on Grand.
Mindport is a half-block on the left.

Film & Art

Features Kid Friendly

Description
Mindport is not a highly-publicized center for learning and the
arts, but it should be. This exhibition space is devoted to provok-
ing thought and inspiring wonder with a hands-on approach that
brings theory into concrete perspective. Mindport opened in
1995 and is free to the public — funding being provided by an
anonymous benefactor.

The building is filled with an interesting blend of science, technology, nature, psychology and anthropology. Many of the
exhibits are science based, much like the Pacific Science Center.
Mirrors that go on for infinity, adjustable distorting mirrors and
rotating kaleidoscopes all encourage the viewer to touch and
experiment with different angles and effects, much like the other
exhibits. Another optical effect that was amazing was a mesmeriz-
ing spiral whose instructions told the viewer to stare at it for ten
seconds and then at another object. Staring at the spiral and then
at a large picture of starfish on the wall made the tentacles seem
to move and contract. There were also math games, puzzles, a
Cartesian diver and a machine that recorded speech and played it
backwards, to name a few. The Ping Pong Ball Express was my
personal favorite — a vacuum tube that sent a ping pong ball
along a hollow tube across the ceiling and along the walls of the
building. Some of the exhibits were too difficult for this reviewer
to figure out, but there is a notebook with answers and instructions for each one.

That is not to say that all of the exhibits were science based.
There was also water sculptures, nature photography, quotes
from Henry David Thoreau, Native American ceremonial masks,
plants of the northwest and measurements of energy consump-
tion of different cultures. Overall, Mindport is an interesting and
refreshing mix of science and nature in an impressive collection
of exhibits that appeal to both adults and children. Groups are
welcome, but the gallery prefers advance notice of groups of
more than six.

Written by Glen Berry

Whatcom Museum

Address
121 Prospect St.
Bellingham WA, 98225

Hours
Tues-Sun Noon - 5:00pm

Directions:
From Holly Street, turn right on
Flora and left on Prospect Street. It's
on the left.

Description
The Whatcom County Museum is
housed in the old City Hall building,
an historic structure in its own
right. Built in 1893, the red brick
building is a Victorian design by a
local architect. Today, the old City
Hall building serves as the main
building for the expanding museum
campus, which also includes the Syre Education Center, Arco
Exhibits and the Whatcom Children's Museum.

The museum sponsors art exhibits, natural history and fund-rais-
ing events. The museum also sponsors gallery walks, walking
tours of the historic buildings of the city, history and art lessons
for local schools and adult groups, and historic cruises on
Bellingham Bay. An active community organization, the museum
offers or sponsors a wide variety of events and workshops for
the local community through its campus. The Whatcom
Museum's staff who are exceptionally knowledgeable about the
area, giving lectures for students, children and visitors on the history of Whatcom County.

The building was renovation in 1999, which involved work on
the housing for the elevator, rebuilt roofs and repair of the
cupolas. The interior has been redone with a clean, modern
gallery look with doors and paneling of native and imported
hardwoods. The first floor houses changing local natural-history
exhibits; the second is of contemporary art; and the third retains
a permanent display of Victorian clothing, woodworking and
toys. The Arco Building contains changing art and history
exhibits as well as the Museum's gift shop and bookstore.

Written by Glen Berry

Syre Center

Address
206 Prospect St.
Bellingham WA, 98225

Hours
Tues-Sun - 5:00pm

Directions:
From Lakeway, go down Holly Street to Flora and turn right. Go left on Prospect. The museum is just past the Whatcom Museum of History and Art.

Features
Kid Friendly, Wheelchair Accessible

Description
Part of the Whatcom Museum's expanding campus, the Syre Education Center is in the old fire hall next to the museum. The center occupies the main floor of the old building and houses three permanent exhibits of the natural history of Bellingham and surrounding areas. Admission is free and the tour is self guided; guides can be requested if arrangements are made in advance.

In the main room is an anthropological display of the First Nations peoples of the north Pacific Coast. One section includes a respectable collection of carved wood chests, tools, ceremonial masks and blankets, which are all representative of the northwest coast tribes. The Inuit part of the display includes woven baskets with geometric designs, tools and carved ivory figurines, among other things.

The European settlement of the region is also documented, with recreated rooms of a settler's cabin c.1890-1900, and a Victorian-style bedroom and parlor. Tools of the settlement years are included, as well as old jars, cookware and butter churns. There are also some excellent photographs of old-growth timber and logging in the northwest, used as background images in the forestry displays.

An entire side of the Education Center is dedicated to an exhibit of birds that are native to the northwest. Once I got over the initial aversion of looking at dead birds, I found the depth of the collection and quality of the specimens amazing. The birds of prey part included many animals you would never have the opportunity to see in the wild, including owls, hawks, eagles and even a vulture. The hundreds of birds are broken down into their natural habitat: sea coast, high mountain and forest, and lowland/farm.

Written by Glen Berry

Film & Art

Lynden Pioneer Museum

Address
217 W. Front St
Lynden WA, 98264

Hours
Mon-Sat 10:00am - 4:00pm

Directions:
Corner of Front & 3rd Downtown Lynden

Description
Set amidst beautiful Lynden, the Lynden Pioneer Museum has many fun and exciting experiences to offer. Be sure to explore the historic downtown area around the museum as you peek into its many shops and learn about the Dutch heritage of the community.

At the museum, one can discover the history of Lynden. Its exhibits span five large and two small galleries, giving you an insight into the settlement and growth of Lynden and the Nooksack valley. The museum also explores the history of transportation from horse to horsepower, and the impact of World Wars I and II, and the Korean conflict on Whatcom County. Take part in classes and workshops or attend tours and presentations that will give you an opportunity to learn about local history — in depth and hands on.

Visitors can look into a full-size pioneer homestead and stroll down a life-size replica of historic Front Street at the turn of the century. Also present is the largest collection of horse-drawn vehicles in the state and a collection of more than 20 vintage automobiles and tractors, some of which cannot be seen anywhere else.

Written by Wayne Berry

Bellingham Theatre Guild

Address
1600 H St.
Bellingham WA, 98225

Directions:
The theatre is two blocks down on the left from Dupont, going towards the water.

Description
The Bellingham Theatre Guild is one of the few places to host community theater productions in the area. Therefore, the BTG is an important member of the diverse arts scene in Bellingham, having a rich, 70-year history of bringing theater to the residents of Whatcom County.

There is a lot more to theater than Shakespeare and the BTG proves it with a variety of productions. Recent offerings by the BTG include musicals, comedies, suspense and drama — both contemporary and classic. The theater's goal is to provide quality productions at reasonable prices, and it certainly accomplishes this with impressive production values and quality acting. For schedules and tickets, refer to the phone number to contact the box office; circulars are usually distributed prior to the opening of a new production. Besides the box office, tickets are available one hour before curtain.

The cast and crew of BTG's half-a-dozen performances per year are comprised mainly of volunteers from the community. A full-time technical director was recently added to the staff to insure consistent quality in the lighting and set design. The BTG traditionally hosts "cold readings" from the script for parts in plays. One of the shining stars to emerge from the BTG is Hillary Swank, star of the movies "Buffy, The Vampire Slayer" and "The Next Karate Kid" and was cast on Fox Network's "Beverly Hills, 90210." For available parts and audition times, as well as additional requirements (singing or improvisational exercises), contact the BTG at 734-5503.

Written by Glen Berry

Film & Art

Video Extreme

Address
1012 W. Holly St.
Bellingham WA, 98225

Hours
Every day 10:00am - 10:00pm

Directions:
From Lakeway, take Holly Street through Old Town. The store is just past F Street by the gas station.

Features
DVD Rentals

Description
"If Blockbuster won't carry it, we will," is the unofficial motto of Jonathan Sims, owner of Video Extreme. This is certainly reflected in the selection of videos, ranging from the uncommon to the bizarre. Since its opening in March of 1994, Video Extreme has amassed an assortment of more than 3000 titles for the film watcher in search of the extraordinary.

The name Video Extreme suggests a collection of fringe and unusual titles, and it certainly does not disappoint. There is an excellent selection of the popular cult genres, such as Japanimation (animé), Kung Fu/Martial Arts and the Mondo Violence/Faces of Death series. The store carries a smattering of underground and independent directors, like David Lynch, John Waters, Terry Gilliam and the ever-popular Ed Wood. Cult action hero's are well represented with Jackie Chan and Chow Yun Fat rarities. Video Extreme also carries the most complete collection of Russ Meyer films I have ever seen, which is impressive in its own right. There is a wide selection of adult titles for those who are 18 years and older.

Also interesting is a complete section of Something Weird titles, a Seattle based distributor that reissues 50's, 60's and 70's B films and soft-core movies. The films are indeed odd ("Hitler's Harlets High School Honeys" was one title), and are guaranteed to amuse the psychotronic crowd. Even further out on the fringe were offerings of experimental and homemade/limited distribution underground titles which you would have to look hard for to ever find again.

Written by Glen Berry

World Premiere Video

Address
1306 Lakeway Dr.
Bellingham WA, 98226

Hours
Every day 10:00am - Midnight

Directions:
It's right across from the entrance to Civic Field in a strip mall with a 7-11.

Features
DVD Rentals

Description
Another of the many video rental houses in Bellingham, World Premiere offers a vast selection of videos and video games. WP is no slouch when it comes to formats, either. They don't have Betamax tapes but they do have VHS and DVD movies. Games for home entertainment systems include those for Nintendo 64 and Sony Playstation.

Within the confines of WP is an impressive library of 15,000 VHS tapes. The large stock of recent releases, which lines the outside wall of the store, is Blockbusteresque in the duplication of popular titles. The usual genres of drama, sci-fi, anime, comedy, etc., fill in the rest of the store. Primarily, the selection is popular fare with a few oddities ("Cannibal Women in the Avocado Jungle of Death") thrown in for good measure. Purveyors of "adult" film will not be disappointed — an 18 and over section exists in the back of the store at the end of a forbidding tunnel. For fans of the good old song and dance, there is an entire section of musicals including (but not limited to) "Hair," "Bye Bye Birdie" and "Madonna: Truth or Dare." For those on the cutting-edge of technology, WP boasts a 600-title collection of DVD movies, with titles ranging from "Armageddon" to "Top Gun."

Gamers will find a large complement of Nintendo 64 and Sony Playstation games to tempt them. Two aisles of titles present themselves for consideration to the energetic teen or the lethargic college student. Whether you're high tech or low brow, you'll find some type of entertainment to fit into your machine at home.

Written by Glen Berry

Film & Art

Film is Truth

Address
1220 N. State St.
Bellingham WA, 98225

Hours
Mon-Fri 4:00pm - Midnight
Sat-Sun 2:00pm - Midnight

Directions:
From Lakeway, go down Holly and
turn left on State Street. FIT is mid-
block on the left.

Description
Named after a well-known quote
(amongst film students, at least)
from Jean Luc-Goddard, "Film is
truth, 24 times a second," is a reference to life captured in the art
of film. As the name would suggest, the video store is devoted to
more eclectic and sophisticated tastes. Film is Truth is an example of video stores that reflect the increasing interest in independent and foreign film, a movement away from the mass-consump-
tion releases found in chain stores.

Independent titles are indeed well represented, with the new-
release section boasting a collection of who's who and what's
what of independent films from the last year or two. Although
there is the occasional mainstream release thrown in, there is an
impressive faithfulness to indie distributors — especially the
well-known and established ones. The organization of the rest of
the 2000-plus videos is alphabetical and is an interesting assortment of films that appeal to a wide variety of tastes.

As one would expect, there are classics, including Hitchcock and
film noir, art-house films, documentaries, foreign and other various and sundry films which fit into no category at all. There is
also the obligatory film-student fare, from Sam Raimi's, "Evil Dead"
to Dziga Vertov's, "Man with the Movie Camera," as well as documentaries profiling directors. Not only does Film is Truth carry a
wide selection for the serious film buff, they also have just-for-fun
Kung Fu, Clint Eastwood classics, old television series, and the
much sought-after rarity, "Cool as Ice."

Written by Glen Berry

Restaurants

The restaurant make-up of the Fourth Corner has certainly changed during the past decade, fueled by population growth and development in the county. A surprising number of cafes and restaurants have sprung up and thrived, each having its own personality. This is one of Whatcom County's charming appeals – the sense of individuality and support of local businesses. Fairhaven and downtown Bellingham are prime examples, exclusively free of chain and fast-food restaurants.

Bellingham has always enjoyed a cosmopolitan reputation, which is certainly reflected in the city's restaurants. Ethnic restaurants are not just a token smattering nor the standard Chinese/Mexican fare — the city has a welcome collection of distinct choices. For some reason, Whatcom County has a fantastic selection of Mexican food places, even though it is as far from the border as you can get. Mediterranean, too, is well represented, from classic pizzerias to exotic Greek eateries. Fans of Asian cuisine will not be disappointed with the choices of Chinese, Japanese, Indian and Thai food.

For those interested in more traditional fare, area restaurants make great use of local products in the classic steak and seafood houses. "Fresh ingredients" and "home made" are popular boasts on menus, backed up by seafood from local waters and produce from nearby fields. In addition, quaint nooks like Old Town Cafe and Green Acres cater to local tastes with all-natural, organic and vegan dishes. In many ways, these one-of-a-kind locations make this area great, if you enjoy new experiences when going out to eat.

In the following section, you will find the best restaurants in the Whatcom County. They have been chosen for their originality and popularity, and, most of all, for their great food. Each offers an original experience, so here's your chance to explore.

Restaurants

Busara

Address	**Hours**

Address
324 36th St.
Bellingham WA, 98225

Hours
Mon 11:30am - 3:00pm
Mon 5:00pm - 10:00pm
Tues-Fri 5:00pm - 10:00pm
Tues-Fri 11:30am - 3:00pm
Sat 11:30am - 10:00pm
Sun 11:30am - 9:30pm

Directions:
Busara is hidden back in Sehome Village, near the south side
Haggen, next door to Roundtable Pizza.

Features
Lunch, Dinner

Description
Busara is a Thai food restaurant tucked into a storefront of the
Sehome Village strip mall. With a contemporary decor, cloth napkins and a very clean feel, this is an excellent place to bring your
date. Both can sit down to a fine dinner amongst a mix of college
students and south-side elite. The night that I was there the
restaurant was busy and — with a very small ante area — many
couples were waiting out of the rain.

The food, however, is worth the wait. Good-sized portions with a
variety of colors and smells typify the Thai cuisine. Also, the ingredients were fresh and the dishes reasonably priced. The Thai
spring rolls — in my opinion the benchmark of a good Thai
house — were made from hand and just crisp enough without
being overcooked. That's a good sign, unlike like other places
which might serve the frozen kind found in a grocery store. The
bathing rama — chicken on spinach with peanut sauce — was
mouth watering. The peanut sauce was excellent; unlike anything
I could have bought at the store.

Busara is the Thai word for blue topaz, and this restaurant is certainly a gem in the rough. Plan to wait on the busier nights.
However, it appears many people were doing take-out.

Written by Wayne Berry

China Gourmet Express

Address
3092 Northwest Ave.
Bellingham WA, 98225

Hours
Mon-Fri 11:30am - 10:00pm
Sat Noon - 10:00pm
Sun Noon - 9:00pm

Directions:
China Gourmet Express is in the strip mall across the street from Yeagers.

Features
Dinner, Take-Out, Lunch

Description
China Gourmet Express, like its name suggests, is a take-out Chinese restaurant with secondary dine-in seating. Signature lunch specials are available at an amazingly low price. With the lunch special you get fried rice, sweet and sour vegetables, soup and choice of 20 entrees.

When eating dinner, I sat at their modest seating and enjoyed the almond chicken and sesame chicken with an appetizer of wontons and barbecue pork. The wontons were very tasty and fresh; the barbecue pork was excellent as well. Unlike the typical florescent red pre-shaped pieces you get at some other Chinese food restaurants (and now some grocery stores), these were hand made, tender and appeared a mild shade of maroon — I would recommend them. The chicken entrees were also appetizing, hearty portions with lots of vegetables.

China Gourmet Express is a blue-collar lunch spot — cheap, delicious take-out Chinese food. Pleasantly, there was no one eating dinner while I was in, making the service very fast — the waitress treated me like royalty. I was also impressed that she wrote down our order in Chinese. On a side note, they do not deliver and they do not take credit cards, so bring your checkbook.

Written by Wayne Berry

Restaurants

Kowloon Garden

Address
4365 Guide Meridian
Bellingham WA, 98226

Hours
Every day 11:30am - 9:45pm

Directions:
From the I-5 Guide Meridian exit, travel north on Guide Meridian for about half a mile. Kowloon Garden will be on the left after Kellogg Road, but before Horton Road.

Features
Dinner, Lunch

Description
The product: Chinese food accentuated with the properties of the Kowloon and Canton regions. The place: Kowloon Garden on the Guide Meridian. The reason: There are too many to explain in one compact sentence, such as the previous ones. Hence, the breakdown:

You generally know what kinds of food you'll find at a Chinese restaurant — they all serve chicken chow mein. So to be successful, these types of restaurants have to one up each other in as many areas as they can. Kowloon Garden does some things well that make people want to go there. First, the food is great. With the recent proliferation of grocery stores peddling a fast-food version of Chinese cuisine, it's refreshing to know you can still go to a real Chinese restaurant. At Kowloon, you will pay about the same price, but you can bet you'll eat a great meal and you'll get more food then you might find elsewhere. The prices are slightly higher than some Chinese places around town, but a combination dinner still costs under $10 with tax and a tip.

You can sit down in a cozy booth, relax, drink tea and listen to an elevator-music version of Led Zeppelin's "Tangerine." You can enjoy the primarily red interior of Kowloon Garden — something different. You can debate with a companion whether or not the origin of graduation tassels began in China (you will see what I mean when you go there). You can get table service from a woman in a silk kimono-like blouse. You can experience all these pleasures when stopping by Kowloon Garden — it is definitely worth a trip out the Guide.

Written by Ken Brierly

Teriyaki Bar

Address
119 W. Holly St.
Bellingham WA, 98225

Hours
Every day 10:00am - 9:00pm

Directions:
Down Holly Street from Lakeway,
The T-Bar is on the left past
Cornwall Avenue and before
Commercial.

Features
Dinner, Lunch

Description
A favorite of the downtown lunch crowd, the Teriyaki Bar offers large portions at lunch prices. The restaurant is modern with a contemporary counter and luncheon tables. The food may be Japanese but the speed and convenience are definitely American, with styrofoam to-go boxes available for those on the run.

The menu is composed mainly of chicken and beef teriyaki and curry dishes, served with steamed Japanese rice and sunomono salad. Serving size on the rice is nothing short of enormous. The sunomono salad is a variation of green salad with shredded cabbage and a sweet, tangy dressing. Chicken is cooked on the bone with their trademark teriyaki sauce. The curries may not look that pretty, but they are quite good, served over a mound of steamed rice. Tasty and a bit spicy, the curry has a mild bite, but not overwhelming. There is also a wide selection of teriyaki burgers, including a vegetarian garden burger. Buckets of chicken are available to go and delivery (with a $10 minimum) is offered free within a three-mile radius.

The ambience is light and bright with high ceilings and hanging plants. Tall bay windows look out on the street and passersby on West Holly. Large, glossy photographs hang on the exposed brick wall inside — images of Asia, Antarctica and the U.S. In both atmosphere and food, the Teriyaki Bar is a mix of Japanese flavor and American sensibility.

Written by Glen Berry

Restaurants

India Grill

Address
1215-1/2 Cornwall Ave.
Bellingham WA, 98225

Hours
Sun-Thurs 4:30pm - 9:00pm
Fri 4:30pm - 9:30pm
Sat 4:30pm - 9:30pm
Sun-Thurs 11:00am - 3:00pm

Directions:
From Lakeway, take Holly Street to
Cornwall and go left. India Grill is
on the right, midblock.

Features
Dinner, Lunch

Description
Despite its cosmopolitan reputation, Bellingham seems to lack
the rich variety of ethnic restaurants that can be found in larger
urban areas, such as Seattle and Vancouver, British Columbia. For
this reason, the India Grill is a welcome addition to downtown
Bellingham. Both a restaurant and full bar, the India Grill offers
authentic East Indian cuisine for lunch and dinner.

Inside the restaurant, diners find themselves seated under a
multi-colored canvas with geometric designs which hangs high
above on the ceiling. As one of my dinner companions remarked,
"You feel as if you are sitting in a tent;" a sentiment easily under-
stood by glancing up at the light filtering through the fabric.
Dark, earthy murals of traditional Indian scenes are displayed on
the walls, as well as tapestries.

The most remarkable thing about the restaurant, however, is the
variety of dishes. Familiar dishes include Tandoori, Nan, Tikki
Masala as well as Boti and Sheekh Kabab — all served with
Basmati Rice. Some of the more interesting choices include Lamb
Vindaloo (leg of lamb in spicy brown sauce and vinegar), Saag
Paneer (homemade cheese with spinach), and Makni Dal (lentils
cooked with butter cream and spices), to name a few. The food
was well prepared and brought sizzling to the table. Curry sauces
were delicate and understated with a light ginger taste — a
pleasant change from other curries, which can be overwhelming
sometimes.

Written by Glen Berry

Lynden Dutch Bakery

Address
421 Front Street
Lynden WA, 98264

Hours
Mon-Fri 5:00am - 6:00pm

Directions:
Exit I-5 at Bay-Lynden Rd (exit 270) and travel eastward 8 miles toward Lynden. Left on 539, then right on Front St. Follow the signs to Dutch Village Mall.

Features
Wheelchair Accessible, Lunch, Take-Out, Espresso, Outdoor seating

Description
A short ramble off I-5 with the Cascades at your nose and Canadian peaks off your shoulder, will bring you to the spruce Dutch community of Lynden. Mt. Baker looms so large there, the town's Little Leaguers could surely smack one right over it's frosty tip. And if you're very lucky, you're heading for the Lynden Dutch Bakery where an unbearably alluring array of home baked cakes, pies, cookies and rolls await you.

This is a "Destination" bakery where "What's Good Today?" is a ludicrous question. These baked goods are folk art where the press of the hand lends signature to the piece and the flavors are flawlessly perfect. Chocolate caramel pie. Cinnamon sticky rolls. Something so simple as a Raisin Bun is perfection. This bakery serves soups and sandwiches as well and you'll find those offerings equally memorable; whomping "Dutch" subs and a medley of soups (pea soup daily)!

The bakery does $15,000 a week in business, with much of the sales in coffee and its most popular item, "Krenten Bolles", those perfect Raisin Buns. Doors open at 5:00 am, a suitable hour for the local dairy farmers whose milking day begins at 4:30. Bakery staff, in floral dresses with white laced aprons and hats attend to the bustle, flinging their native Dutch tongue about in good natured sass and humor. A playful spirit prevails here with the available pie flavors grouped by frequency: "Always" (Dutch Apple, Bumble Berry, Strawberry Rhubarb and Chocolate Caramel), "Sometimes", and "Never Again" (Pickle).

At the Lynden Dutch Bakery, it's the sign over the counter that expresses it best: "There's no place like this place anywhere near this place so this must be the place!" Enter into the calories with wild abandon, as maybe, just maybe, this is how life is best lived.

Written by Debra Exley

Restaurants

Tony's Coffees

Address
1101 Harris Ave.
Bellingham WA, 98225

Hours
Mon-Thurs 7:00am - 9:00pm
Fri 7:00am - 9:30pm
Sat 7:30am - 9:30pm
Sun 7:30am - 9:00pm

Directions:
From I-5 and Old Fairhaven
Parkway, turn right on 12th Street
and left on Harris. Tony's is down
one block on the corner.

Features
Breakfast, Lunch, Smoke-free

Description
Tony's Coffee House was the first
place I went in town when I came
to Bellingham four years ago to
check out Western Washington
University. The down-to-earth
atmosphere, eclectic staff and
clientele probably had as much to do with my final decision to
come here as anything else. Located in the heart of old
Fairhaven across the street from the fabulous Village Books, it's
a great place to escape for an hour or two and enjoy a latte
and biscotti. The collection of worn chess sets have received
countless hours of my attention as well. Tony's has undergone
a few face-lifts since my first visit, most noticeably the opening
of the Harris Avenue Cafe in it's upper section, but that same
eclectic feel is there. Hardwood floors, big bay windows and
old style stained glass porticos give the place a warm, homey
feeling that seems to appeal to most everyone.

The main reasons for going to Tony's are the coffees and teas,
of course. The dry coffee and tea outlet has been moved downtown proper, but you can still get the wet kind here. The
barista whips up some unique and interesting concoctions in
the espresso department, using Tony's own Orca Espresso
Blend. Beyond the traditional lattes and mochas lie options like
the exotic Moroccan; a mocha made with unsweetened chocolate, providing a mellow alternative to the heavy sweetness of
your average mocha. Then there's my personal favorite, the
Fantasia; a mocha with a thick slice of orange squeezed and
left in the cup. They've even got several frozen drinks,

whipped up before your eyes in classic soda-jerk style. Tony's tea selection features 58 different types, including products from Tony's own label, Celestial Seasonings and Twinnings. They also carry six medicinal selections.

The Harris Street Cafe, which opened in October of 1998, offers a tempting breakfast menu featuring delicious omelets, pan fried red potatoes, crepes and all the standard morning fare. Their lunches consist largely of hot and cold sandwiches, soups and salads, as well as a limited cold menu after 2 p.m. And even though it's got a separate name and a fresh paint job, the Harris still carries Tony's old charm and relaxed atmosphere. The expansion has simply added one more reason to visit this popular locals retreat.

Written by Dave Shepherd

Restaurants

Cafe Toulouse

Address
114 W Magnolia #102
Bellingham WA, 98225

Directions:
The cafe is housed in the Crown Plaza, right next to the post office downtown.

Features
Dinner, Lunch, Espresso, Smoke-free

Description
The name "Café", it seems, has been appropriated by half the restaurants in town. The definition is ambiguous and covers a wide range of styles, tastes and fares. However, if there was ever a restaurant that deserved the name, it is the Café Toulouse. The Café Toulouse not only earns the name but defines it— serving as the epitome of "café" with class and distinction.

I freely admit that in the past, I had avoided the café. From the exterior, it has the upscale look that draws upscale people who can afford upscale prices for upscale food. The sign in the window advertising "wood-fired pizzas" reinforced my mistaken impression, and mistaken impression it was. The interior is indeed classy, with small wooden tables and a marble tiled counter facing the kitchen island. Suit-and-tie clientele dine under Toulouse-Lautrec reproductions, the café's namesake. The atmosphere is quiet and restive but does not discourage conversation. However, the wait staff takes none of this for granted, serving with warm friendliness and quiet courtesy.

With all these pleasant surprises, it would be easy for the menu to fall short of expectations. On the contrary— the selection is tempting, prices are reasonable and the food is superb. Choices include the light fare one would expect of a good café: pasta, sandwiches, salads, entrees a la carte and the signature wood-fired pizzas. Of course, coffee and espresso are served as well. Pastas are sautèed with white wine and salads are served bursting with color and a myriad of fresh ingredients.

The moral to this story is: Do not to be fooled by misconceptions. They only prevented me from discovering this delightful café which is bound to be a regular destination.

Written by Glen Berry

Green Acres

Address
4 Prospect Street
Bellingham WA, 98225

Hours
Every day 9:00am - 4:00pm

Directions:
Travelling east on Lakeway, Holly Street meets Lakeway at the Ellis and Lakeway intersection. Holly Street is a main thoroughfare through downtown Bellingham. As you come down Holly, Prospect Street will be on your right, after Commercial Street.

Features
Kid Friendly, Delivery, Lunch, Take-Out, Breakfast, Espresso, Outdoor seating

Description
Walking into Green Acres' Restaurant is an instant replay of how the '70's was lit — with funny, funky and downright tacky lamps. The walls of this smallish, campy café are lined with shelves displaying memorabilia from the 1950s to the 70s, including table lamps, display trays, cookie jars and, interestingly, snack tray sets. (Check out the back of the menu for an explanation!) This is definitely a come-as-you-are, casual kind of place, appealing to twenty-something artists, neo-beatniks and students. Seating consists of retro tables and chairs, with a small bar along the window offering an excellent vantage point for people watching. Outdoor service is also offered, a few tables and chairs along the sidewalk near the entrance.

Green Acres serves breakfast and lunch. Breakfast choices include egg scrambles, buckwheat hotcakes, and straw potato leek cakes. The lunch menu offers an array of salads, soups, quiche, and chicken, veggie- and fish burgers. The fish burgers are made on the premises, with no additives or preservatives. Also available is an espresso menu, tea and soft drinks. The Mexi Burger, consisting of a generous-sized veggie burger, cheese, green chilies and avocado on a multi-grain bun, came with a side of blue-corn tortilla chips, and, while not inspired, was quite edible. We also tried a croissant sandwich, being two eggs on a croissant along with a choice of additional ingredients — the mix of Canadian bacon, avocado and Swiss cheese that we tried was particularly good. Both items were generously portioned and — here's the part the cheapskate in me digs — quite inexpensive. For a filling breakfast or lunch at retro prices, Green Acres is indeed the place to be.

The restaurant strives to support local farmers, obtaining produce and dairy from Washington state growers. Free delivery is offered in the downtown area, with a $10 minimum order.

Written by Tanya Perkins

Restaurants

Sidewalk Cafe

Address
655 Front St.
Lynden WA, 98264

Hours
Mon-Thurs 7:00am - 6:00pm
Sat 7:00am - 6:00pm
Fri 7:00am - 8:00pm

Directions:
Drive north on Guide Meridian to Lynden. Turn right onto Front Street, and follow road (and signs) to the Dutch Village Mall. The restaurant is located right inside the main entrance.

Features
Breakfast, Dinner, Lunch, Catering, Espresso, Wheelchair Accessible

Description
The Sidewalk Cafe is not on a sidewalk, as one might expect, but instead sits inside Lynden's Dutch Village Mall. Even so, the cafe's decor certainly gives the impression of outdoor sidewalk dining. Patio tables and sun umbrellas speckle the cafe's floor space; many are placed conveniently alongside the indoor canal, allowing customers to watch the swimming fish while enjoying their meal. For those that prefer people-watching, gift shops and galleries are located across from the cafe for buyers and window-shoppers to wander through.

The sign at the Sidewalk Cafe boasts "good home cooking." This claim is easily tested with the first bite of thickly sliced soft bread used for sandwiches such as turkey and cream cheese, roast beef, ham and cheese, vegetarian, and the like. Sandwiches come in half or whole sizes (look for daily specials), and each is served with the customer's choice of soup, french fries, potato salad, or a garden salad. In addition to the cold deli sandwiches, the cafe offers a selection of salads, including taco salad, caesar salad, and an oriental salad, and some hot dishes as well. Fat scones and cookies tempt from behind the glass case— a perfect snack with a cup of hot espresso. The cafe also has a breakfast menu available for early-morning customers, which offers selections ranging from egg, sausage, and toast combinations to Belgian waffles and pancakes.

Lynden's Dutch Village Mall displays this town's fervor for its rich Dutch heritage. The Sidewalk Cafe fits in well with the setting, and its quiet, conservative feel provides a nice break for shoppers anticipating a good deli sandwich, some hot soup, or a simple cup of coffee. Those visiting the mall should make this restaurant a regular stop, whether it is their first visit, or their fiftieth.

Written by Kimberly Baer

Colophon Café

Address
1208 11th St.
Bellingham WA, 98225

Hours
Mon-Sat 9:00am - 10:00pm
Sun 10:00am - 8:00pm

Directions:
From Old Fairhaven Parkway, go right on 12th Street, left on Harris Avenue and right on 11th. Colophon is on the left, mid block.

Features
Breakfast, Lunch, Outdoor seating

Description

It would be safe to say that the social nucleus of Fairhaven can be pinpointed somewhere within the walls of the Colophon Café — perhaps near the old elevator downstairs or beside a bookshelf. The café shares space with Village Books on Harris Avenue and offers people a place to meet, converse, read books and dine. The powerful attraction of good food and books has made it one of the most popular places in Fairhaven.

There is no real separation between bookstore and café. Upstairs, there is only a partial wall between the counter and booths of the restaurant and the bookshelves. Downstairs, the main dining area is sandwiched between the two other parts of the bookstore, with patrons of both businesses intermingling. The downstairs offers dining at tables with a maitre d' and menus. This area is often quite busy and humming with conversation. The upper level serves more as a quick stop for those who want coffee or dessert, the '50's-style soda fountain stools and booths occupied by book readers and coffee drinkers, for the most part. My favorite quirk about this unique restaurant is the hollow tube in the counter upstairs that workers use to call down to the kitchen. The person above can then use the dumb-waiter behind the counter to bring food up from below.

The lunch and dinner menu is composed of soups, salads and sandwiches. Turkey, chicken, fish, ham and veggie combinations are offered on bagel, Russian rye, wheat and sourdough breads. There is an interesting selection of soups to choose from: African Peanut, Mexican Corn & Bean and Clam Chowder being a few. Soups change daily, but there are monthly calendars for those who want to plan ahead. I personally recommend the homemade desserts — they alone are worth the trip. The desserts are big enough (and rich enough) for two. A partial list includes Chocolate Chunk Cake, Irish Crème and fruit pies, cobblers, turnovers and several different cheesecakes.

Written by Glen Berry

Restaurants

Old Town Cafe

Address
316 W. Holly St.
Bellingham WA, 98225

Hours
Mon-Sat 7:00am - 3:00pm
Sun 8:00am - 2:00am

Directions:
Go down Holly St. to where it merges into a two way street and
the Old Town Cafe is right there on the right nestled between
some antique shops.

Features
Breakfast, Lunch

Description
Many eateries feel the need to have some hook or gimmick to
draw in patrons. The only hook The Old Town Cafe seems to
need is an honest approach to making good food that will appeal
to everyone. Located at the northwestern end of Holly Street in
downtown Bellingham, the Old Town serves up breakfasts and
lunches with broad appeal daily.

The Old Town is a true local's establishment. Not too ritzy and
not too earthy, the Old Town blends a warm, clean, comfortable
atmosphere with a classic menu that draws heavily on all-natural
products and organic produce from local providers. But the cafe
doesn't shove its commitment to healthy, natural foods in your
face. You probably won't even notice you're eating better, save
the wholesome quality and enhanced flavor of every dish they
serve.

It's the little touches, however, that really show Old Town's community focus. The owners utilize the wall space to display and
sell works by local artists. They have a long communal table
where you can get to know other diners. Local musicians can
pop in and earn themselves a free meal for impromptu performances, provided they play for an hour, but will still get a free
beverage if they only perform a couple of songs. And big kudos
are in order for the extra-wide ramp between the upper and
lower parlors, which makes the restaurant wheelchair friendly.

One word of warning: The Old Town Cafe is a breakfast hot spot
for locals on the weekends, so on Saturdays and Sundays you can
expect a 15- to 20-minute wait.

Written by Dave Shepherd

Cookie Cafe´

Address
1319 Cornwall Ave.
Bellingham WA, 98225

Hours
Sun-Tues 6:00am - 6:00pm
Wed 6:00am - 9:00pm
Thurs 6:00am - 9:00pm
Fri 6:00am - 10:00pm
Sat 7:00am - 10:00pm

Directions:
Traveling down Holly Street, turn right on Cornwall Avenue.
RB's Cookie Cafe is located near the middle of the block on the
left-hand side.

Features
Banquet Facilities, Lunch, Smoke-free, Wheelchair Accessible

Description
RB's Cookie Cafe´ offers a lot more than just cookies. It is a
bakery, a coffee shop, an eatery and a venue for live entertainment. A longtime resident on Cornwall Avenue, going out for
coffee is synonymous with going to the Cookie Cafe´ for many
who work downtown. The Cookie Cafe´ has moved a few doors
down the block next to the MB Green plant store. This location
has enhanced the atmosphere of the Cookie Cafe´, as the non-
smoking dining area and plant store are not separated by a wall
and customers may look at the exotic foliage and passersby on
the street.

The Cookie Café was serving espresso and gourmet coffee
before it was trendy, so they know the secrets to achieving a
good cup of joe. Fresh, homemade soups are available every day,
and often, soup choices include a vegetarian blend. Lasagna, chili,
baked potatoes, quiche and deli sandwiches are also popular and
delicious items. However, as the name suggests, be sure to try a
cookie or other baked item —- you will never buy from the
supermarket again.

If you are starving to death or need a mocha but you can't break
away from work, the cafe´ will deliver the order at no charge
($5 minimum order) in the downtown business district. They
also provide group luncheons or baked goods for group events.
The cafe´ also boasts a group facility for up to 85 people. On
some occasions, RB's Cookie Cafe´ books musicians and other
aspiring local entertainers. Considering Bellingham's lack of
music venues, the Cookie Cafe´ is an important part of the local
music scene.

Written by Ken Brierly

Restaurants

Flying Dutchman

Address
608 Front St.
Lynden WA, 98264

Directions:
Heading north on Guide Meridian, drive straight into Lynden and turn right onto Front Street, which leads directly into the main downtown area.

Features
Espresso, Smoke-free, Kid Friendly, Lunch, Take-Out

Description
The Flying Dutchman Coffee House offers a casually rumpled alternative to the windmills, wooden shoes and delft blue accents of downtown Lynden. This means no disrespect to Lynden's downtown but, let's face it - it does have a serious case of the cutes. Anyway, despite its name, Wagner fans, the Flying Dutchman has no tall ships or cases of unrequited love (well, who knows). Instead, you will find professional sports banners, Dilbert T-shirts, Pooh toys, footballs, puzzles, model planes and an array of offbeat Monopoly games including the Harley Davidson, NASCAR, Dairy (that's right) and U.S. Space Program versions. The variety of items displayed on the walls and shelves gives a fun spirit to the Flying Dutchman and makes it a hit with kids. For mom and dad, the coffee house also sells Pike Street's famous Market Spice Tea by the box.

The edible offerings at the Flying Dutchman are basic: salads, subs, sandwiches, soup du jour, chili, hot dogs, milkshakes, fruit smoothies, ice cream, cookies, muffins, biscotti, espresso and specialty lattes. The soup du jour on the day I visited was beef noodle, which my daughter loved. This alone makes it worthy of comment, since she is a toddler and thus resistant to all food not chocolate. We also tried the vegetarian sandwich on whole wheat which was really good - the veggies were very fresh and crunchy, with just the right amount of cream cheese. We topped it off with a giant, saucer-sized chocolate chip cookie. All in all, it was a pleasant lunch at a reasonable price.

Seating in the Flying Dutchman consists of eight tables or so, with old church pews along two walls in the front. The place is easy to find on Lynden's Front Street, being located beside the "Postkantoor" (post office for those of you rusty on your Dutch), with a rack of fluttering windsocks outside the front door.

Written by Tanya Perkins

Harbor Cafe

Address
295 Marine Dr.
Blaine WA, 98230

Hours
Every day 6:00am - 10:00pm
Sat-Sun 10:00am - 2:00am
Mon-Fri 11:00am - 2:00am

Directions:
From Peace Portal Drive in Blaine turn west on Marine Drive
The Harbor Cafe will be on your left about a 1/2 a mile down
the street.

Features
Wheelchair Accessible, Breakfast, Lunch, Beer and Wine, Dinner,
Sunday Brunch

Description
The Harbor Café is located just minutes from the Peace Arch
crossing in Blaine. The restaurant features stunning views of the
Peace Arch and the water. Don't be surprised if you see a whale
surfacing. If you don't see a live whale, you can take an easy stroll
to Marine Park and play on the killer whale sculptures, beach
comb during low tide or take a short ride on the historic Plover
Ferry to Semi-Ah-Moo.

The Harbor Café menu features a little something for everyone.
Selections range from breakfast items like omelets and combinations featuring French toast, eggs and bacon or pancakes to lunch
and dinner selections such as a variety of seafood, burgers and
sandwiches. The fried foods tend to be a little on the greasy side,
but that helps to brings out the flavor. They even have reduced
portion meals for those who don't want to be too stuffed. A good
variety of white and red wines are also available at the table or
for other selections guests can visit the Last Set Lounge. The
restaurant has distinct smoking and non-smoking areas, but non-
smokers may still notice the odor of smoke. If you have room
after your meal, the friendly staff will direct you to the Harbor
Café's grand dessert case where you should be able to find
something to satisfy you sweet tooth. Reservations are not
required, however they are accepted and you may want to
consider making them if you have a large group because the
restaurant is very popular.

Appropriately named, the Harbor Café is situated on the water,
within easy access of fishing and recreational boating opportunities. It has a nautical decor with large anchor out front and
marine artwork adorns the walls inside. You can even take a little
of the restaurant home as the artwork may be purchased. So If
you're looking for a good, fast meal, on your way to or from
Canada, look no further than the Harbor Café. You may even get
to see a whale!

Written by Dave Erickson

Restaurants

Skylark's

Address
1308-B Eleventh Street
Bellingham WA, 98225

Hours
Every day 7:00am - 10:00pm

Directions:
The cafe is tucked away in the back of the old Fairhaven Post Office building on Eleventh Street, In the heart of Fairhaven. From the corner of Harris Avenue and Eleventh Street, walk one half block down the hill on Harris, turn left onto the cobblestone path. The entrance to Skylark's is at the top of the rise in the path.

Features
Kid Friendly, Breakfast, Espresso, Outdoor seating, Beer and Wine, Dinner, Lunch, Take-Out

Description
One of Fairhaven's better kept secrets is Skylark's "Hidden Cafe." Skylark's is worth seeking out for a hearty lunch or dinner, a handmade milkshake on a hot summer afternoon, or a chocolate grand mariner mousse after watching a glorious sunset over Bellingham Bay.

During the summer season, outside seating is available on the winding cobblestone beneath the shade of the large chestnut tree, giving the cafe a European feel. Inside the cafe, natural light pours through the large West-facing windows illuminating a simple but elegant updating of Fairhaven's historic architecture: brick and natural wood accents, a small wood stove with dancing flames and framed reproductions of vintage artwork.

Two unique soups are featured each day. With over fifty soups offered each month, ranging from Asian Vegetable Tofu to Wild Mushrooms and Cream, Skylark's helpfully publishes a monthly calendar. Between 7 am to 11 pm, breakfast ranges from the basic eggs, hashbrowns and pancakes to a Mediterranean Frittata filled with black olives, spinach, tomato, feta cheese and baked to perfection.

Lunch and dinner bring even more variety. Sandwiches vary from a reinvented peanut butter and jelly—or banana—to a "Greek" sandwich, with crumbled feta cheese, tomato, cucumber, red onion on hearty black rye bread. Hot sandwiches include a very tasty reuben on dark rye, and a "garden" burger served with cucumber, sprouts and stone ground mustard.

Salad lovers also need to bring a hearty appetite. The caesar salad with its fresh romaine lettuce, grated parmesan and zesty croutons, accompanied by a freshly baked whole wheat roll, is nearly a meal for two.

A nice selection of pasta dishes round out the menu, offering seafood combinations, vegetarian and non-vegetarian entrees. I found the Penne Marinara, with its rich tomato sauce filled with green peppers, mushrooms, garlic and onion, does indeed fulfill Skylark's promise about its great pasta: "We never skimp on the portion."

Desert may not be "doable" after a Skylark's meal, but consider a return trip to check out the bourbon bread pudding or the peach cobbler. Or, if like me, you are a "slave" to chocolate, what better choice than the chocolate decadence with raspberry puree.

Written by Rob Olason

Restaurants

Lafeens

Address
1466 Electric Ave
Bellingham WA, 98225

Hours
Mon-Fri 5:00am - Midnight
Sat 5:00am - 2:00am
Sun 5:00am - Midnight

Directions:
It's right across from the main entrance to Whatcom Falls Park next to the minimart.

Features
Breakfast, Smoke-free

Description
It's safe to say there aren't a whole lot of places open past 10 p.m. in Bellingham. That is, places that aren't filled with smoke, pinball machines and neon beer signs. Lafeen's bakery is one of those few places. However, to describe it as a bakery would be to limit the possibilities this establishment offers.

The first thing one notices when entering Lafeen's is the large glass counter which separates the wide-eyed children from the pastries on the other side. The array is breathtaking: gigantic fritters, maple bars, turnovers, twists and raspberry-filled, bear claw and old fashioned donuts. There are also cookies and muffins to tempt those who can get past the arsenal of donuts. If donuts aren't your thing, Lafeen's also offers a freezer of ice cream and frozen yogurt, as well as sundaes and milk shakes made on the spot.

To go along with all those pastries is the obligatory coffee in the diner-standard pots as well as an espresso machine. Milk is available, as is hot chocolate for the cold days. A battery of juices presents itself for the health conscious who were dragged into this den of sugar iniquity. This is truly an eatery of the locals. Business cards plaster one section of the wall and post cards cover another. Early in the morning, the donut shop is the domain of the elderly and commuters on their way to work. During the afternoon, Lafeen's is the territory of school children that crowd the picnic benches of the restaurant. The late night/early morning crowd at Lafeen's tends to be the college students poring over books or the punk rock kids with no place else to go.

Written by Glen Berry

Stuart's

Address
1302 Bay St.
Bellingham WA, 98225

Hours
Sun-Thurs 7:00am - Midnight
Fri 8:30am - Midnight
Sat 8:30am - Midnight

Directions:
From Lakeway, take Holly Street
down to Bay Street. Stuart's on the
right.

Features: Espresso, Smoke-free

Description
Everything that you've ever wanted
in a coffee shop can be found down-
town at Stuart's Coffee House. A favorite of the young adult and
college crowds, Stuart's bills itself as, "Your downtown living
room." The coffee shop is indeed comfortable and low key;
employees took no notice of me as I wandered about scribbling
notes.

The coffee shop is in an old building which adds a lot of character to the place. The wood floors, Persian rugs and exposed brick
walls give the coffee shop a rustic feel. Small, wooden tables sit in
front of large windows, each with its own small, brass lamp. In
addition, there are Victorian-style couches, plush chairs and an old
player piano. There are also the classic staples: a chessboard, a
bookshelf with books and a bulletin board filled with posters of
local musicians, poets, writers and sketches by the patrons.
Soothing jazz music plays over the sound system as patrons sit
quietly, reading and sipping espresso from the small coffee bar.
The bar offers the typical fare of coffee, tea, cold beverages,
bagels, and other lunch and dessert items. A balcony above the
coffee shop offers a partial view of the bay and waterfront.

Evening events are also held here, including poetry readings, chess
matches, storytelling, and live jazz and other music. Poetry slams,
which have become popular in recent years, are held every fourth
Monday of the month. Owners plan on bringing in art exhibitions
again in the coming months; a Democracy Café, discussing the
current political system in the U.S., is to be announced.

Written by Glen Berry

Restaurants

La Pinata

Address
1317 Commercial St.
Bellingham WA, 98225

Hours
Fri 11:00am - 1:30am
Sun-Thurs 11:00am - 10:00pm
Sat 11:00am - 1:30am

Directions:
From Lakeway, take Holly Street to Commercial Avenue and turn right. It is mid block on the left.

Address
1125 Sunset Dr
Bellingham WA, 98226

Directions:
It's smack dab in the middle of Sunset Square, right next to the theater on the K-mart side.

Features
Beer and Wine, Dinner, Full Bar, Karaoke, Lunch

Description
Witnessing upstart Mexican restaurants explode in Whatcom County during the past few years, it is clear that purveyors of south-of-the-border cuisine want a piece of the huge success that La Pinata has enjoyed during its many years in Bellingham. A veritable titan in this niche, La Pinata has endured, and even flourished, in the face of competition. Not only has this establishment managed to keep its downtown location bustling, but it has expanded to better serve its north Bellingham customers via a newer location at Sunset Square retail center. The key for La Pinata is simple:

The portions are generous, delicious and inexpensive and the service is fast and friendly. For less than $10, diners receive more food than can possibly be eaten during one sitting. Waiting for a table is also a rarity, despite the place's popularity. Seldom, if ever, does an order take more than 10 minutes to arrive at the table. However, while waiting for the main course, diners receive a complimentary basket of homemade tortilla chips and the hottest salsa north of Tijuana. Even if you don't have a penchant for a burnt tongue, the food is worth the wait. La Pinata also offers a mind-boggling selection of margarita choices, daiquiris, Mexican and domestic beers, and any other potion you may desire from its complete bars.

La Pinata's downtown location has a few more amenities than the Sunset branch. The atmosphere of the downtown restaurant has a more traditional feel with its painted stucco and high ceilings, whereas the Sunset location has a more modern aesthetic. Both locations also feature bar-room karaoke some nights of the week and downtown's has a banquet room upstairs for larger gatherings. In the bar — at either location — patrons can check out the big game on one of the television screens.

Written by Ken Brierly

Casa Que Pasa

Address
1415 Railroad Ave.
Bellingham WA, 98225

Hours
Sun-Tues 11:00am - 11:00pm
Wed-Sat 11:00am - 1:00am

Directions:
Going down Holly Street, go right for a block-and-a-half on Railroad. Casa's on the left, across from the WTA terminal.

Features
Beer and Wine, Full Bar, Outdoor seating, Wheelchair Accessible, Dinner, Lunch, Take-Out

Description
When I first walked into Casa Que Pasa in 1992, there wasn't much there. The floor was clean and there was a cook, but that is all that could be said about the atmosphere. What they did have was a huge burrito for a great price. A lot of things may have changed with Casa Que Pasa, but there is one thing that certainly hasn't — three-fourths pound medium burritos and one-pound jumbos for prices that won't break the bank. Although the menu is mainly populated by burritos, patrons also have tacos, fajitas, chimichangas and quesadillas to choose from. Casa Que Pasa offers vegetarian fare — both meat-free and vegan (completely free of meat juices or oils, cooked on separate surfaces).

The atmosphere of Casa Que Pasa is festive and community oriented, with the obligatory bulletin board for event postings. Local art graces the walls, as well as a gigantic mural over the front windows. Tables are painted with brilliant suns and other colorful designs. There is an attempt to inject some south-of-the-border flair in the form of a classic, fake tropical bird hanging from the ceiling. Also, Latino music sometimes plucks the sound system, but, overall, Casa Que Pasa has more of a Bellingham feel to it than Mexican.

A relatively recent expansion has brought a Mexican cantina to the back of the restaurant which boasts "50 tequilas for your agave enjoyment." In case you do not know, Mexican law requires a minimum of fifty-one percent of the spirits in Tequila must be derived from the cactus-like, blue agave plant — only found in the Jalisco region of Mexico. There is no Mexican law regarding the worm — at least that I'm aware of. The cantina also offers daiquiris and a variety of ales.

Written by Glen Berry

Restaurants

Bandito's Burritos

Address
120 W Holly St.
Bellingham WA, 98225

Hours
Mon-Fri 11:00am - 10:00pm
Sat 11:00am - 9:00pm
Sun - 9:00pm

Directions:
Bandito's Burritos is on the first
floor of the parking garage on Holly
Street; just remember that Holly is a
one way street down the hill, and
you can go wrong. Across from the
US Bank.

Features
Dinner, Take-Out, Lunch

Description
If you're on a budget and you want to get the full value of your
dollar when it comes to Mexican food, look no further than
Bandito's Burritos. Tucked into the corner of a building on Holly
Street, Bandito's appears to be made to order for the downtown
lunch crowd. However, the sheer immensity of the burritos make
it hard to believe anyone could consume a whole one for lunch.

The interior of Bandito's is bright and clean with large glass windows and hints of southwest U.S./Mexican décor. However, this is
not the main attraction. It is the aforementioned gigantic burritos.
There are certainly other items on the menu (Tacos and
Quesadillas), but they seem more of an afterthought. The Jumbo
is the recommended entry-level item on the menu. Burritos come
with rice, red or black beans and salsa, but it is all conveniently
wrapped in a shell for carry-out orders. If you're looking for an
early morning pick-me-up, give the breakfast burritos a try.
Breakfast burritos come in differing combinations of eggs,
potatoes, beans and cheese mixed with a heart, sweet red salsa.
Burritos are assembled in front of you by a young, friendly staff.
Bandito's is also health conscious, using low-fat vegetarian beans,
lean meats, low-fat dairy products and high-fiber rice. Also,
Bandito's does not grill or deep fry any of its dishes so diners
can eat well with a clear conscience.

Also noteworthy is the surprising selection of salsas which change
daily with at least six offered on the table next to the counter.
Examples include Fresh Red, Zesty Red, Kitchen Sink, Sweet Heat,
Peanut Jalapeno, Garlic Lover's and Punch Pineapple. Each comes
rated Wimpy, Mild, Getting Warmer, Fire and Toxic. Also of interest
is free delivery of burritos with a minimum $7 purchase.

Written by Glen Berry

Chihuahua

Address
5694 3rd
Ferndale WA, 98248

Hours
Sun-Thurs 11:00am -10:00pm
Sat 11:00am - 11:00pm
Fri 11:00am - 11:00pm

Directions:
From Main street in Ferndale, take a right onto third. The
Chihuahua is right down the street on the corner.

Features
Dinner, Take-Out, Beer and Wine, Lunch

Description
There is something so tongue-in-cheek about the Chihuahua
Family Restaurant. It is a Mexican restaurant distinctly aware that
it is far from Mexico. It seems to cater more to the
Northwesterner's idea of Mexico than to authenticity. A smart
move, and one so tastefully executed that the blend of Mexican
and American cuisine and decor appears seamless. Even the name,
Chihuahua, is exotic but familiar on the Northwestern tongue.

The food is serious business here. You can expect to be served
Carne Asada, Carnitas de Res, Huevos con Chorizo in portions so
large your stomach will surely hurt should you choose to clean
your plate. The salsa is tangy and a bit spicy, but five-alarm it is
not. The pico de gallo is fresh and compliments just about anything you order. If your children refuse even the tamest of
Mexican fare, the Chihuahua offers burgers and fries. Lunch and
dinner specials are available, as well as takeout. Perhaps the most
extraordinary thing about the menu is the relatively wide range of
vegetarian dishes it boasts. Spinach Tamale, Mole en Hongos and
Burrito Relleno, among others, are novelties to most visitors. All in
all, the menu is quite extensive, including beer, wine, mixed drinks
and desserts.

The service, as well as the decor, is unobtrusive. Both compliment
your dining experience rather than distract from it. You can
expect to enjoy your meal surrounded by a Tex-mex scene, complete with terra cotta and colorful murals. The tables are topped
with a distinctly Southwestern design, foreign enough to the
Fourth Corner to be exotic. The service is attentive but if
hovering waiters delight you, the Chihuahua isn't going to be your
hot spot. Far from pushy, the servers here are capable of removing
your plates and refilling your drinks without even a pause in your
conversation.

If you want a little bit of Mexico, the Chihuahua can certainly provide it. With reasonable prices and accommodating hours, this is
the restaurant for Sunday brunch, afternoon lunch with the girls
or your buddies from work, and a Saturday night dinner with your
spouse.

Written by Holly Gray

Restaurants

Gloria's

Address
2400 Meridian St.
Bellingham WA, 98225

Hours
Every day 11:00am - 10:00pm

Directions:
Gloria's has relocated to the heart of
the Fountain District near the intersection of Broadway and Meridian,
in the old Fountain Bakery location.

Features
Beer and Wine, Lunch, Dinner

Description

The competition amongst Mexican food restaurants in
Bellingham is fierce, to say the least. For aficionados of South-of-
the-Border cuisine, this town offers seemingly no end to choices
of excellent restaurants with eight offerings and new additions
on the way. Despite the saturated market, Gloria's is arguably the
best, with great food, a family atmosphere and good value.

The fare is familiar: enchiladas, tostadas, burritos and
chimichangas. The manner of preparation is referred to as Jalisco
style and is served smothered in red sauce and cheese.
Conventional wisdom suggests that this type of Mexican food is
best washed down with a margarita or imported Mexican beer.
As with all good Mexican restaurants, meals are prefaced with a
basket of chips and two different types of red salsa. Most plates
come replete with a generous helping of excellent fried rice and
refried beans. Combinaciones grandes are indeed huge — you'd
better unbuckle your belt if you plan on consuming the whole
thing. Unless you have a huge stomach (or ego), I'd recommend
going for the small combination or the single items. In any event,
make sure to save room for the wonderful sopapilla — a dessert
of light, flaky tortilla and whipped cream, maraschino cherries
and corn syrup.

The attribute that distinguishes Gloria's from the field of com-
petitors (aside from the great food) is its reputation as a family
restaurant. This is not PC veggie burritos and 1001 Margaritas
aimed strictly at the college crowd. It is run by a family and
patronized by families. The large, hand-carved wooden benches
are spacious, the music is authentic and the atmosphere is comfortable. This is a place to sit down, relax and have a great meal.

Written by Glen Berry

Carol's Coffee Cup

Address
5415 Mt. Baker Highway
Deming WA, 98244

Directions:
Head out the Mt. Baker Highway for 14 miles until you reach
Deming, then start looking on the right for the sign with the
steaming coffee cup above the small diner.

Features
Breakfast, Espresso, Outdoor seating, Dinner, Lunch, Take-Out

Description
A parking lot is frequently a reliable indication of whether or not
a restaurant is any good. The fuller the lot, usually, the better the
food. When we pulled into Carol's Coffee Cup's parking lot one
recent wet Tuesday afternoon, the lot was almost full. Parking lots
rarely lie and this one was bang on - pointing to a very busy
restaurant serving very good food. Carol's Coffee Cup is a small,
homey nook of a restaurant whose interior gives every indication
of having remained unchanged for decades. This is not pseudo
retro - this is the real thing. And so is the food.

Despite its name, Carol's Coffee Cup serves lots of things beside
coffee. Lunch and dinner offerings include salads, soups and sandwiches as well as sturdier fare, like huge hamburgers and chicken
fried steak, and comfort food, like macaroni and cheese and
turkey dinner, one of the most popular items on the menu. The
mushroom burger was wonderful - packed with flavorful sautéed
mushrooms, bacon and Swiss cheese. The turkey dinner was
authentic, complete with homemade dressing, mashed potatoes,
gravy and cranberry sauce. We also tried the onion rings, which
were good, and topped it off with a chocolate shake - the old
fashioned kind which is so different from fast food fare. Breakfast
is also served and includes pancakes, omelets, bacon, sausage and
cereal.

Carol's Coffee Cup has seven booths, a couple of tables, counter
service, and a small outdoor patio. Its the kind of place where the
servers and the regulars are on a first-name basis and the butter
that comes with your roll is a plop of real butter, not a rigid,
paper-wrapped cube. It is worth the 20 minute drive from
Bellingham to eat at a place that recalls simpler times and cooks
up food like grandma served.

Written by Tanya Perkins

Restaurants

Ferndale Bakery

Address
5686 Third Avenue
Ferndale, WA 98248

Hours
Mon-Sat 6:00am - 5:30pm

Directions:
Take the Ferndale 262 exit and proceed west. Corss over the Nooksack River and go to third Avenue. Turn right on third. The bakery will be mid-block on your right.

Description
If you have a pension for pound cake, a craving for cookies or a desire for doughnuts then the Ferndale Bakery is for you. Conveniently located in downtown Ferndale, the Ferndale Bakery boasts some of the best aromas, friendliest staff and most colorful conversation in town.

As a destination for morning coffee the Ferndale Bakery can't be beat. Join locals to find out what is happening in the city and indulge yourself in some of the most appetizing and fattening treats the city has to offer (just don't tell your doctor!). From rolls and bread, to cookies and pastries, you can't go wrong with any of the made from scratch selections.

Claire and Michael Beilner, the owners of the bakery, are active community event sponsors. You will often find their bakery goods at civic or a variety of other functions. An example of this commitment to the community is the fund raising effort they are undertaking to raise money for downtown lighted decorations. The bakery is selling cookies to raise funds for this endeavor. It this community spirit, combined with a friendly staff that makes this small town bakery a big hit.

The bakery is also the perfect choice for your large event or occasion. Your choice of food can make or break your meeting or special occasion. The Ferndale Bakery takes the guesswork out this task. Wedding cakes that melt in your mouth and the large variety of pastries and doughnuts won't leave you or your guests disappointed. Prices are reasonable, but smelling the fresh baked bread is free. On street parking is limited however, which sometimes makes getting into the bakery more challenging. There is plenty of parking located in a large parking lot behind the bakery on Second Avenue.

Take the time to follow your nose to the Ferndale Bakery, just make sure you leave your diet behind.

Written by Dave Erickson

Bagelry

Address
1319 Railroad Ave.
Bellingham WA, 98225

Hours
Mon-Fri 6:30am - 5:00pm
Sat 7:30am - 4:00pm
Sun 8:00am - 3:00pm

Directions:
The Bagelry is on Railroad Avenue between Holly
and Champion streets.

Features
Breakfast, Lunch, Outdoor seating

Description
Anyone who has walked down Railroad Avenue is familiar with
the heavenly smell that wafts out of The Bagelry, torturing hungry
passersby. The large front windows offer a look inside to the ever-
present book readers and coffee drinkers occupying the wooden
tables and front counter of the restaurant. The business is separated into two sides; one side for orders to go and one side for dining. High ceilings and overhead fans give this bright breakfast
eatery an airy, open feel.

As the name would imply, the focus of the Bagelry is hot, fresh
bagels baked New York style from a secret recipe carefully guard-
ed by the owner. Care is taken in the preparation of the bagels,
and this special attention is reflected in the superior quality of
the final product. Dough is hand rolled, "proofed," boiled and
baked. Bialy (pronounced "be-ah-lee") style bagels are offered as
well and are a variety of bagel without a hole; they are not boiled
before they are baked. Despite the appeal to more sophisticated
tastes, the prices of bagels are more than reasonable.

Novice bagel consumers may find themselves overwhelmed by
the selection of bagels, not to mention the cream cheeses.
Choices range from the more common raisin/cinnamon, blueber-
ry and whole wheat bagels to pumpernickel, salted and bialy
bagels for those with more eclectic tastes. Connoisseurs will not
be disappointed with exotic cream cheeses like lox, sun-dried
tomato and basil, scallion and a feta cheese/garlic/dill combination. Other breakfast items are included on the menu, including
omelets, espresso and baked goods.

Written by Glen Berry

Restaurants

Horseshoe

Address
113 E. Holly Street
Bellingham WA, 98225

Hours
Open 24 Hours

Directions:
From Lakeway, take Holly Street to downtown. The Horseshoe is on the right after Railroad Avenue and before Cornwall.

Features
Beer and Wine, Breakfast, Dinner, Full Bar, Lunch

Description
If you come back to the same restaurant three times and you feel like you're a stranger, the restaurant is doing something wrong, according to owner Jack Kahn. The Horseshoe certainly evokes a particular affection in anyone who has spent time within its smoky confines. The Horseshoe was established (according to the sign) in 1886, and is billed as Bellingham's version of Cheers. It may be a long way from an upscale Boston watering hole with its Texas Longhorns and western art, but it is certainly a place where everybody will get to know your name.

The green naugahyde seats in their faux wood frames are a matter of pride, as well as the wood carvings that were designed by Duff Tweed, one of the original designers of Disneyland. The menu is consistent with the retro feel of the restaurant, consisting mainly of traditional American fare of the 40's and 50's diner. As an acknowledgement to the college crowd, veggie burgers and a few other hip items have been added to the menu. I found myself watching my P's and Q's with the waitress, who seemed more like a friend's mother than a waitress — another testament to the down-to-earth feel of the Horseshoe.

The Ranch Room, a separate part of the establishment where the hard liquor is served, is the main attraction at the Horseshoe on a Friday or Saturday night. The close quarters of The Ranch Room certainly make for an intimate get-to-know-your-neighbor atmosphere, if only out of sheer proximity. Because it is open all night, the Horseshoe also serves as a favorite place for the bar hopper's end of the night meal. You would be hard pressed to find a more interesting place (besides St. Joseph's Emergency Room) at 3 a.m. on a Friday.

Written by Glen Berry

Little Cheerful

Address
113 E. Holly St.
Bellingham WA, 98225

Hours
Mon-Fri 7:00am - 3:00pm
Sat-Sun 8:00am - 2:00pm

Directions:
From Lakeway take Holly Street to
Railroad Avenue. The Cafe is on the
right at the intersection.

Features
Breakfast, Outdoor seating,
Smoke-free

Description

The Little Cheerful is perhaps the most popular breakfast eatery
in downtown Bellingham. Aptly named, the Little Cheerful has a
casual, friendly atmosphere and staff. Upon entering the restaurant, one sees a old-fashioned dinner counter separating diners
from the grills on the opposite side, cooking the huge mounds of
hash browns the restaurant is famous for. The majority of patrons
choose to sit at the small, intimate wooden tables that line the
narrow restaurant.

Although the menu does have sandwiches, The Little Cheerful is
first and foremost a meeting place for breakfast. The fare is clas-
sic-American breakfast food, with bacon, eggs, sausage, muffins,
etc. Vegetarians have the option of ordering the house specialty,
veggie browns. Hash browns come in two sizes — very large, and
more than one person can possibly eat. I personally recommend
the half order because even the largest of my college buddies
cannot finish a whole order. The price is right too, with a great
value for everything on the menu.

The Little Cheerful is understandably popular because of its great
food and large portions. The restaurant is especially frequented
by college students for these reasons. Getting a seat in the restaurant can be difficult on the weekend; late Sunday morning is
impossible, so plan accordingly.

Written by Glen Berry

Restaurants

Mannino's

Address
130 E. Champion St.
Bellingham WA, 98225

Hours
Every day 11:30am - 2:30pm
Every day 5:00pm - 9:00pm

Directions:
Take E. Holly Street to Railroad Avenue, turn right. Take Railroad Avenue for two blocks (via the parking lot) until you reach Champion Street. Manninos is on that corner.

Features
Dinner, Lunch, Takes Reservations

Description
Mannino's Italian Restaurant is an oasis of continental Italian cuisine tucked neatly away from the bustle of downtown Bellingham. Although it's a mere two blocks from East Holly Street, Mannino's provides a taste of old Italy with a refreshing, elegant style. The clean, black and white checkered floor of Mannino's glows under the flickering candles that adorn the 16 glass-top tables. The aesthetic qualities of Mannino's pales only in comparison to its variety of delicious pasta and seafood dishes, such as stuffed jumbo shells, linguine, and seafood-pasta meals.

Mannino's semiformal atmosphere is conducive to being a great place to impress a date or an important business client. Mannino's has an extensive wine list to accompany dishes and a full bar. A courteous wait staff will take your jacket at the door and graciously fill your appetizer order or get you a drink from the bar while you wait for your meal. When consuming one of Mannino's plentiful portions of pasta, keep in mind that an impressive menu of authentic Italian desserts awaits.

The cozy, smoke-free setting and quality of food at Mannino's means reservations are recommended, especially on weekends. Lunch begins at 11:30 a.m. and dinner seating runs until 9 p.m., 7 nights a week. Parking is plentiful in the evenings but diners may have to park in the nearby metered lots during the day. So if your can't afford the airfare to Italy but you still want to experience the elegance and good food, Mannino's may be the place for you.

Written by Tyler Watson

Cafe´ Akroteri

Address
1219 Cornwall Ave.
Bellingham WA, 98225

Hours
Mon-Sat 11:00am - 10:00pm
Fri 11:00am - 2:00am
Sun 4:00pm - 9:00pm
Sat 11:00am - 2:00am

Directions:
On Cornwall, across from the
Leopold Hotel.

Features
Kid Friendly, Beer and Wine, Full Bar, Outdoor seating, Take-Out,
Wheelchair Accessible, Dinner, Lunch, Smoke-free,
Takes Reservations

Description
There's a slice of the Greek Islands in downtown Bellingham,
right across the street from the Leopold Hotel. It is called Cafe´
Akroteri. They have a large parking lot and it is offered to their
patrons free of charge. (It's so nice to not have to concern
yourself about a parking meter while you eat!) Should the sun
ever shine, there is an outdoor area with covered tables and a
patio feeling adjacent to the restaurant.

The large dining room is bright and airy, partitioned for sound,
but open for light, with views of the downtown streets. The Old
World art that ranges the room is highlighted by track lighting;
ingeniously used to host ivy vines which also conceal cords to
lamps over each table. While the main dining room is smoke free,
those who choose may turn right and find a full bar that is as
bright, with views of the downtown Bellingham area and with
meal service throughout the day. (Light menu is served after 10
PM.) Each meal comes with lightly toasted French bread that is a
joy to behold. Criminally fresh and warm, it competes with your
entrée for attentions of the palate. There are meat and vegetarian
entrees, as well as soups and salad for the diet conscious. The
Greek Salad consist of large pieces of real vegetables; olives,
tomatoes, cucumber, green onion, green pepper and feta cheese;
no lettuce. You'll know you've actually eaten something.

The prices are very reasonable, certainly competitive for lunch
and for dinner. Wines are available at the table, both imported
and domestic.

The staff here is very friendly and steeped in Old World charm
themselves. This certainly is a conducive place for meeting
friends or doing business in a relaxed and informal environment.

Written by Shelagh Considine

Restaurants

Lucci's Pizzeria

Address
2615 Harbor Loop
Bellingham WA, 98225

Hours
Mon-Thurs 11:30am - 8:00pm
Fri 11:30am - 10:00pm
Sat 11:30am - 10:00pm
Sun 1:00pm - 9:00pm

Directions:
From Lakeway, go Down Holly Street through Old Town and turn left on F street. Across the tracks, go right on Roeder for a couple miles and turn left on Coho. At the end of the road, you'll see the restaurant on the left.

Features
Beer and Wine, Dinner, Full Bar, Lunch, Takes Reservations

Description
Names can be deceiving. For example, the name of Lucci's Bayshore Pizzeria doesn't convey the full story of what they have to offer. Situated on Bellingham's waterfront at the northern-most harbor, Lucci's Bayshore Pizzeria serves up a wide array of cuisine, including seafood, meat-and-potato dishes and other standard American fare. But they have a penchant for Italian cuisine, as they are known for their delicious pizzas, salad and pasta dishes. Be warned: One may think that they have become The Godfather while partaking of Lucci's Italian food, but this effect is only temporary and should wear off within a couple hours after the dining experience is complete.

Lucci's also offers a maritime atmosphere that is second-to-none. The two-tiered restaurant overlooks the portion of the harbor that is primarily fishing boats and touring vessels. The downstairs portion of the restaurant is spanned by an impressive system of salt-water fish tanks that are connected by glass tubes allowing the sea life to mosey from tank-to-tank. The atmosphere is elegant, but not pretentious – a casual diner at Lucci's is as common as the dressed-up couple on a date.

Lucci's features a cozy circular bar, similar to that of Cheer's fame. Again, one can expect eclectic clientele while sipping at the bar – salty fishermen, fisherwomen, elegant couples and Seattle Mariner fans catching the game on one of the televisions have all been known to pull up stools next to each other. Reservations are recommended but not required. Lucci's Bayshore Pizzeria is located next to the Bellingham Yacht Club.

Written by Ken Brierly

Syros

Address
311 Front
Lynden WA, 98264

Hours
Every day 11:00am - 11:00pm

Directions:
Entering Lynden from the west take Front Street. Syros will be on your right near the end of downtown.

Features
Wheelchair Accessible, Beer and Wine, Full Bar, Takes Reservations, Banquet Facilities, Dinner, Lunch

Description
What's the last place in Whatcom County you would think of to find authentic Italian and Greek cuisine? If you guessed Lynden, you're right! Surprisingly, Lynden hosts one of the tastiest Italian and Greek eateries anywhere. Syros Greek and Italian Restaurant is located near the end of Front Street in downtown Lynden.

Syros features real authentic menu items such as Spankopita, Rigatoni, Spaghetti, Roast Lamb, Moresaka and much much more. Generous appetizers and a salad bar compliment one of the most complete Italian menus you'll find anywhere. The restaurant also has other selections such as steak, ribs and chicken for those who may not be in the mood for Mediterranean. Syros has a full service lounge which features a big screen TV and separate entrance. The atmosphere of the restaurant is wonderful with soft music, friendly staff, good lighting, an abundance of hanging plants and greenery to go with light colored wood furniture. The restaurant can accommodate large groups in a semi-private back room and will work with guests on special select menus for events such as banquets, parties and rehearsal dinners. Contact Ethie to arrange for your group function. If you would like to give food as a gift, Syros also has gift certificates available. Prices are average and are reasonable for the portions you receive.

So whether you're looking to take a load off you feet after touring the many shops in Lynden, are loading up on carbohydrates for the big race, have a craving for good Italian or Greek food or are planning a large event, take the time to stop in at Syros Greek and Italian Restaurant. You'll be glad you did.

Written by Dave Erickson

Restaurants

Mykonos

Address
1650 W. Bakerview Rd.
Bellingham WA, 98225

Hours
Mon-Thurs 11:30am - 10:00pm
Sat 11:30am - 11:00pm
Fri 11:30am - 11:00pm
Sun 12:30am - 10:00pm

Directions:
Mykonos is located right behind Hampton's Inn near the airport.

Features
Beer and Wine, Lunch, Dinner, Takes Reservations

Description
For many years, the Bellingham airport area has been sorely lacking in dining spots. Since the region surrounding the airport has grown, the opening of Mykonos Greek Restaurant has helped fill that niche. Conveniently located near Interstate 5 behind the Hampton Inn, the restaurant draws business from the airport, the Interstate, and the nearby hotels. Owners Karen and Dimitri Pantoleon have the savvy necessary for success as restaurateurs, having run Syros in Lynden for 12 years. By building Mykonos from scratch, they were able to create a dining spot with a uniqueness all its own.

Enter the upscale eatery and experience a taste of the Mediterranean. To the lobby's right is a bar; straight-ahead is a receiving area where a friendly host or hostess is ready to seat you. To the left is the spacious dining room that seats 120 and is regularly filled each day at lunch and dinner. Diners are surrounded by a luxurious, high-ceiling interior with Corinthian columns and statues, creating a romantic atmosphere.

Mykonos, named after a Greek island, features authentic Greek fare. Dimitri is a native of Tripolis, Greece and uses many family recipes learned from his mother and sister. The delicious pita bread is made fresh in house daily and goes well with the mouthwatering, garlicky humus appetizer. Traditional dishes include moist, tender chicken or lamb souvlaki; zesty Greek salad; sumptuous vegetarian moussaka (eggplant and zucchini); or briam (oven-roasted vegetables with feta cheese and a light, savory tomato sauce). Lunch and dinner prices are reasonable, especially considering the generous portions served.

Written by Nancy Steele

Dimitri's

Address
2113 Main St.
Ferndale WA, 98248

Hours
Mon-Thurs 11:00am - 10:00pm
Fri 11:00am - 11:00pm
Sat 11:00am - 11:00pm

Directions:
Take the Main Street exit from I-5 north. Turn right onto Main
Street. Follow Main Street for approximately 3 miles.
Dimitri's is on the left.

Features
Dinner, Lunch

Description
Dimitri's Greek and Italian Restaurant in downtown Ferndale is a
pizza-lover's heaven. Thirty-two different pizzas are available to
diners. Everything from just a simple cheese pizza to pizzas covered with shrimp, mushrooms, green peppers, onions, salami, arti-
chokes and lean beef is available. Dimitri's also has a variety of
vegetarian pizzas. The clean and spacious Dimitri's — previously
named Contos' Pizza — has many well-padded booths for diners
to enjoy pizza or appetizers after the big game, or just to relax
and talk with old friends. The well-lit restaurant reminds one of
the Mediterranean coast, a place where good food and relaxation
is a priority in life.

Besides having one of the best pizza menus in town, Dimitri's
boasts a wide variety of appetizers, salads, sub sandwiches,
steaks, seafood, burgers, pastas and desserts — a menu which
lends itself to any taste. For those not confident enough to
attempt downing the 12-ounce New York steak, the "Mermaid
Kitchen" may provide a way out. The "Mermaid Kitchen" cooks
up prawns, kalamaria and fish with a Greek flair. Appetizers
include everything from onion rings to authentic Greek food.

Dimitri's is very accessible for the disabled, as the gently sloped
walkway to the restaurant is smoothly paved and not stepped.
Reservations are not necessary. Dimitri's is open daily for lunch
and dinner. They also deliver within a five-mile radius. Dimitri's is
a short drive for those who desire a taste of the Mediterranean.

Written by Tyler Watson

Stanello's

Address
1514 12th St.
Bellingham WA, 98225

Hours
Mon-Fri 4:00pm - 10:00pm
Sat 4:00pm - 11:00pm
Sun 11:30am - 10:00pm

Directions:
Take I-5 exit 250 (Old Fairhaven Parkway) and travel east on the parkway for about one mile to 12th Street. Stanello's is the beige building on the corner of Old Fairhaven Parkway and 12th Street.

Features
Beer and Wine, Dinner, Full Bar, Lunch, Outdoor seating, Takes Reservations, Wheelchair Accessible

Description
Skeptics of change need not worry. Stanello's Restaurant has been tossing great pizza pies for Bellingham residents for nearly a quarter century. Formerly known as Venus Pizza, the owner changed the name to better reflect the restaurant's Italian menu. Also, a more modern location was constructed about five years ago just down the street from its former spot in Old Fairhaven.

Even with these minor changes, Stanello's award-winning pizzas continue to rake in the hardware. Most recently, the pies were voted Best Pizza in Whatcom County in 1994 and 1995. Don't be misled: this isn't some hole-in-the-wall pizza place. Stanello's is a fine-dining establishment that just happens to serve a great pizza. Consider if awards were given for other Italian foods: Stanello's would probably win the bulk of those as well.

Delicious and affordable ravioli, spaghetti, manicotti and chicken cacciatore are some of the classics to choose from. Soup or salad and garlic toast comes with the meals, which average under $10. Choice steaks, fettuccines, and gourmet salads are other tasty options. Also, the dining room is smoke free, but if you care to smoke, have dinner in Stanello's huge bar – complete with 16 televisions. Patrons may also enjoy their favorite appetizers, such as deep-fried mozzarella and jalapeno poppers.

Written by Ken Brierly

D'Anna's Cafe´

Address
1319 N. State St.
Bellingham WA, 98225

Hours
Sun-Fri 4:30pm - 9:00pm
Tues-Fri 11:30am - 2:30pm
Fri 4:30pm - 10:00pm
Sat 4:30pm - 10:00pm

Directions:
Turn west from I-5's Lakeway exit.
Turn right at the forth stoplight.
Turn left on Magnolia. Go one block
and turn right on State Street.
D'Anna's is on the right side of the
street.

Features
Dinner, Lunch, Smoke-free, Takes Reservations

Description
D'Anna's Cafe´ Italiano has mastered the art of pasta making.
Its owners not only fill wholesale pasta orders for exclusive
restaurants in the region, but they offer the traditional tastes of
Italy at their Bellingham restaurant. Handmade daily, D'Anna's
pasta dishes provide a generous portion of food at a reasonable
price; salad and bread are included with lunch and dinner
entrees. Diners may order beer and wine with their meals - and
don't forget the tiramisu; D'Anna's has some of the best desserts
this side of the Old Country.

D'Anna's most popular item is the ravioli. Several varieties of
ravioli are available: One flavor is the spinach, chardonnay, cheese
and local mushroom ravioli; also try the meat, spinach,
Chardonnay and cheese blend; or get the ricotta, romano and
parsley mix. Customers have the option of ordering a dish with
all three ravioli varieties. All entrees are served with salad and
bread before the meal. The salad consists simply of greens and
D'Anna's own vinaigrette. The bread is also unique. It is baked flat
and topped with tomato sauce, cheese and herbs.

Sandwiches, chicken dinners and homemade Italian sausage
dishes are delicious, but get the ravioli. D'Anna's Cafe´ Italiano
is a rather quaint restaurant with somewhat limited seating.
Table seating is available, as are bar stools at a counter. From the
stools, diners can watch the chefs work their culinary magic, and,
occasionally, the patron gets the opportunity to chat with them.
Take-out is also available and can be ordered by phone or fax.

Written by Ken Brierly

Restaurants

Conto's Pizza

Address
825 Peace Portal Dr.
Blaine WA, 98230

Hours
Every day 7:00am - 9:00pm

Directions:
Conto's Pizza is located on Peace Portal Drive in
downtown Blaine.

Features
Wheelchair Accessible, Breakfast, Kid Friendly, Outdoor seating,
Takes Reservations, Beer and Wine, Dinner, Lunch, Smoke-free

Description
A great way to end a day of beach combing at Semiahmoo is to
head to Contos Pizza and Pasta Restaurant in downtown Blaine.
What immediately strikes you about the place is the friendly
atmosphere, the tasteful decor, and, best of all, the huge windows
overlooking the harbor and the San Juan Islands.

Since it was a beautiful summer evening the day I was there,
I chose to sit outside at one of the three stone tables on the
grassy lawn to enjoy my meal and the great view.

I was impressed by the extensive choice on the menu:
Mediterranean pasta dishes, Greek specialties like Mousaka,
Gyros, or Kalamari; pizza with a huge selection of toppings;
seafood, good old-fashioned burgers, BBQ chicken or ribs, not to
mention salads, appetizers and steaks. I took some time to decide
what I was in the mood for, but in the end I could not ignore my
craving for salami pizza and a cold beer. I also ordered a small
Greek salad to get my greens. The beer arrived in a chilled glass;
the pizza arrived, steaming hot, abundant in slices, and with a
blanket of fresh mozzarella cheese over the salami. The salad was
freshly made with wonderful feta cheese and juicy tomatoes. My
companion tried out the beef Gyros on Pita bread with Tzaziki
and a salad. Portions are filling without being overly generous
and are fairly priced. The service was friendly and efficient.

As we sat there enjoying our meal and the sunset, I almost felt as
if I were sitting somewhere in the Greek Islands. Great
Mediterranean food to match a beautiful Western Washington
view. What a match!

Written by Hilary Higgins

Cicchitti's Pizzeria

Address
115 E. Holly
Bellingham WA, 98225

Hours
Every day 11:00am - 10:00pm

Directions:
It's at the corner of Holly and
Railroad, right between the Little
Cheerful and the Horseshoe.

Features
Dinner, Lunch

Description
One cannot really talk about pizza in Bellingham without refer-
ring to Cicchitti's. They are famous for their authentic thin crusts
and homemade sauce, more commonly referred to as "New York
Style" pizza. Family owned and operated, Cicchitti's has been serving pies to the people of Bellingham since 1983. Formerly located on State Street, the restaurant now occupies a space on Holly
Street in the heart of downtown.

A real Italian pizzeria is hard to find, much less one that uses a
hand-thrown Neapolitan crust. They use a family recipe and all
the pies are made by hand. Gigantic wedges of pizza are sold
by the slice, a lunch and dinner time favorite. Whole pies are
available in 18- and 13-inch rounds in the Neapolitan crust and
16-inch squares of the traditional, twice-raised Sicilian crust.
The authenticity doesn't breakdown when it comes to the toppings, with capocolla, pepperoni, salami and Mancini sweet-fried
peppers being a few of the choices available.

Although the pies are enough attraction for most folks, the pizza
just skims the surface of the menu. Italian cuisine aficionados will
not be disappointed by an assortment of dishes that includes
pasta, stromboli and calzones — not to mention soups and
salads. In keeping with the East Coast touch, Philly cheese steak
sandwiches and other hoagies are also featured on the menu.

One has certain expectations of a family pizzeria and Cicchitti's
certainly delivers. The prices are reasonable, the pies are huge
and the staff (read: the family) is amiable and neighborly.
After a few visits to Cicchitti's, you'll feel like you're part of
the family, too.

Written by Glen Berry

Restaurants

Cascade Pizza

Hours
Every day 11:00am - 11:00pm

Address
1120 Lakeway Dr.
Bellingham WA, 98226

Directions: From I-5's Lakeway exit, travel east for a half-mile. It is on the right across from the baseball field.

Address
1825 Riverside Dr.
Mt Vernon WA, 98273

Directions: I-5 South to Mt. Vernon.

Address
2431 Meridian St.
Bellingham WA, 98225

Directions: To find Cascade Pizza on Meridian just look for the restaurant in the Fountain District where all the police cars are parked.

Features
Beer and Wine, Catering, Dinner, Full Bar, Lunch

Description
It's a shame that marketing reasons demand concise names for businesses because too often the name of a great restaurant cannot tell the entire story. Such is the case with Cascade Pizza: Though it does toss a great slab, the name represents only one of its outstanding products.

In a Utopian society where name length had no limits and the size of signs were not bound by zoning restrictions, Cascade Pizza would require a much larger sign outside its Lakeway Drive and Meridian Street restaurants, which might read something like, "Cascade Pizza Featuring Bellingham's Best Crust, Planet Earth's Best Lasagna and Unofficial Hangout For Whatcom County's Law Enforcement Officers." However visionary that name may seem, it is accurate.

If you are like most pizzavores, you devour every part of the pie until you reach its indestructible crust, which you then cast off either to your trained-to-beg-for-crusts dog or to pile by the fireplace to use for kindling. But Cascade's pizza crust is not only edible, it is something to look forward to while you chew your way through the toppings — just be careful not to choke yourself in a mad sprint to reach the crust. If blockage in the esophagus does occur, chug a generous portion from your soft drink pitcher — after all, refills are free-of-charge.

Among its many lasagna choices, the pepperoni lasagna is best. Cascade's is not only excellent lasagna, but the portion is generous. Along with the salad and garlic bread you'll receive before the oven-baked, personal dish arrives, ask for a doggy bag and prepare to get rolled out of the restaurant in the wheelchair you'll need to bring.

On account of all the cops that frequent it, the Meridian location is probably one of the safest places to eat — provided you don't drink too many cocktails and crack an ill-advised donut joke to one of Whatcom County's finest.

Written by Ken Brierly

Le Chat Noir

Address
1200 Harris Ave.
Bellingham WA, 98225

Hours
Mon-Fri 11:30am - 2:00pm
Sat 5:00pm - 11:00pm
Sun 4:00pm - Midnight
Mon-Fri 5:00pm - 11:00pm

Directions:
Drive west on Old Fairhaven Parkway. Turn right on 12th. Le Chat Noir is three blocks down on the corner of 12th and Harris, on the third floor of the Sycamore Square Building.

Features
Beer and Wine, Full Bar, Takes Reservations, Dinner, Lunch

Description
Above Fairhaven sits the symbol of the black cat, silently watching the goings-on of the streets below and the water beyond. The intimate restaurant it marks affords its patrons the same view, while transforming this corner of Bellingham into an intriguing and somewhat eccentric French alleyway— complete with drooping dark green plants and iron fences. Modeled after the original cabaret opened in Paris in 1881, Le Chat Noir is a restaurant with an artistic and mysterious feel. Oh, for the stories these walls could tell.

The atmosphere at Le Chat Noir is equaled only by the food, which is not the common menu standard you might find elsewhere. Here there are bacon-wrapped water chestnut appetizers (a personal favorite–they're more addicting than you think!) and large dinner crepes stuffed with seafood, vegetable and cheese combinations. I tried a Greek salad mounded with crumbly feta cheese and kalamata olives, with a cup of the soup du jour: corn chowder. The chowder, not too thick and creamy as I anticipated, consisted of a light, spicy broth with corn, potatoes, and long strings of melted cheddar in every bite. In addition to the crepes, salads and soups (clam chowder and French onion served daily), Le Chat Noir also offers several chicken dishes, pizzettes, pastas, and tender cuts of steak. Surely there is something here for everyone.

The prices, while higher than those at casual restaurants, remain extremely reasonable for the excellent food and experience they provide. This place is a great excuse to get dressed up for a drink at the bar or to celebrate an intimate dinner. So go to Le Chat Noir for the food or the view if you must, but if for no other reason, go to experience the ambience. It's like none other I've found in Bellingham.

Written by Kimberly Baer

Restaurants

Pacific Cafe´

Address
100 N. Commercial St.
Bellingham WA, 98225

Hours
Mon-Fri 11:30am - 2:00pm
Mon-Sat 5:30pm -

Directions:
Located next to the Mt. Baker Theatre, on the corner of
Commercial and West Champion

Features
Lunch, Takes Reservations, Smoke-free, Wheelchair Accessible,
Beer and Wine, Dinner

Description
With a lot of attention to detail and a mellow ambiance, one look
at the wine list will convince you that you did right in assuring
there was 2 hours in your parking meter. This is definitely a place
to go slow and savor every moment. It is tucked in below the Mt.
Baker theatre, and offers a reclusive haven from the hustle and
bustle of downtown activity. Some Western and Oriental influence prevails on the décor. The lunch menu offers nearly as
much as the dinner menu, with pastas and salads added.

The Appetizers are Fried French Brie, Grilled Portabello
Mushrooms, Dungeness Crab Cakes, Alaska Spot Prawns and
Calamari. Entrees include Breast of Chicken Satay, Mediterranean
Eggplant & Portabello Marinara, Spot Prawns Punjabi Curry, Fresh
King Salmon, and a Tenderloin with 5 Peppercorn Merlot Sauce
that is to die for. Pastas are Tomato Basil Penne, Garlic & Ginger
Chicken Linguine, Pacific Seafood Linguine and Alaska Prawns
Linguine. Salads are a Spicy Calamari, Ginger Marmalade Chicken,
Alaskan Spot Prawns and Honey Glazed Walnuts.

If all that doesn't whet your appetite, the rest of the plate will.
It is a visual delight. The vegetables are treated with dignity, and
the sauces are exciting and flavorful; spicy in a delicate way.

The wines are offered on the list as Interesting Varietals, Red,
White and Desert Wines. The Pacific Cafe´ also has a Reserve List;
Imported or Domestic. They have broken the list down so well
that it makes ordering a bottle for inclusion to dinner an easy
feat. It is obvious that they consider wine a fine accouterment to
dining. While they have an extensive wine list, they also offer
beers and non-alcoholic beverages.

The Cafe opens for dinner at 5:30 PM, but will close depending
on business. It is highly recommended that if you plan to dine
late, make a reservation.

Written by Shelagh Considine

Wild Garlic

Address
114 Prospect
Bellingham WA, 98225

Hours
Mon-Fri 11:00am - 3:00pm
Mon-Sat 5:30pm - 8:00pm

Directions:
The Wild Garlic is downtown across from the
Whatcom Museum.

Features
Beer and Wine, Lunch, Takes Reservations, Kid Friendly,
Smoke-free, Wheelchair Accessible, Dinner

Description
Anywhere in the southern part of downtown (near the museum)
the smell of roasting garlic tells you there is a delightful
restaurant nearby. The restaurant has its' own parking lot so it's
easy to pull in and give way.

Its' name is 'Wild Garlic' and the décor is sumptuous and
comforting. In shades of green highlighted by brick and wood,
the walls are lined with photographs of nature. Mellow jazz plays
in the background, and the lighting is low, adding to a cozy
feeling. Booths add to a feeling of privacy, although tables are also
available. Ropes of garlic adorning the walls remind you of its'
name.

The prices are a pleasant surprise. Moderate is the best way to
explain them, although inexpensive for the environment.

They offer pizza: Garlic, Smoked Salmon, Chicken Artichoke. In
the way of salads: Simply Garlic, Chicken Waldorf, Caesar, Grilled
Chicken Caesar, Rock Shrimp, Garlic Greek. Sandwich options
include Pork Tenderloin, Garlic Chicken, BLT, Garlic Veggie.
The selection of pastas are equally intriguing with choices of
Mediterranean Linguine, Chicken Fettuccine, Smoked Salmon,
Ginger Garlic Shrimp Linguine, Roasted Hazelnut Fettuccine.
They claim the burgers are the towns' best! Add all the goodies
you want to these. Soups are hearty and robust. Don't miss the
specials written daily on a chalkboard. All entrees are served with
hot bread, and salads come with an individual bottle of balsamic
vinegar.

While they cater to the lunch crowd downtown, they also open
in the evenings to serve dinners. They suggest a reservation at
dinner, and at lunch if your party is larger than 4. While they
happily serve children, they have no special menu for them. They
serve Beer, Wines, Soft drinks and Coffees. We can't even begin to
go into the dessert menu, but it is enticing. (Leave some room.)
You know you have found a special place when you are so comfortable in one, and 'Wild Garlic' certainly makes you feel welcome and wonderful.

Written by Shelagh Considine

Restaurants

Marina

Address
985 Thomas Glenn Dr.
Bellingham WA, 98225

Hours
Every day 11:30am - 2:35pm
Every day 5:00pm - 9:00pm

Directions:
From Lakeway, take Holly Street through Old Town and go left on F Street. Across the tracks, turn right on Roeder Avenue. Thomas Glenn Spit is about a half mile down on the left. The restaurant is at the end of the spit.

Features
Beer and Wine, Catering, Dinner, Full Bar, Lunch, Outdoor seating, Takes Reservations, Wheelchair Accessible

Description
Located on the tip of the Thomas J. Glenn spit at Bellingham's waterfront, The Marina Restaurant provides a breathtaking setting for the ideal date, business lunch or entertaining visitors from out of town. Walled by windows, diners can indulge their eyes with panoramic views of the San Juan Islands, a forest of sailboats in the harbor, kite-flyers at Zuanich Point Park and the city's lights.

The Marina is as famous for its food as it is for its setting. Local seafood favorites include king salmon, halibut, oysters, steamed clams and calamari. The Marina also rotates various tropical seafood onto their menu throughout the year. Pastas, choice steaks and salads are also popular menu items. The Marina has a full-service bar as well as a rotating stock of Washington, California and international wines. The bar is located centrally in the restaurant, and those who stop by for a couple cocktails also benefit from the stunning views. The Marina is renowned for its classy service in a classy setting. The staff is friendly and the prices are reasonable – dinner prices start around $10 and average under $20.

The floor plan of the restaurant is such that there is not a bad seat in the house – a view from everywhere. Another business venture of GTM, the long-time local restaurant management company (founders and former owners of The Cliffhouse, Top of the Towers, Dirty Dan Harris' and Sarducci's, to name a few, The Marina's owners take fine dining seriously. Reservations are recommended but not required.

Written by Ken Brierly

Il Fiasco

Address
1309 Commercial
Bellingham WA, 98225

Hours
Sun-Thurs 11:30am - 2:00pm
Sun-Thurs 4:30pm - 9:00pm
Fri 11:30am - Midnight
Sat 11:30am - Midnight

Directions:
Traveling down Holly Street, turn right on Commercial Street. Il Fiasco is near the middle of the block on the left-hand side.

Features
Dinner, Full Bar, Lunch, Takes Reservations

Description
Many misinformed folks fail to consider Il Fiasco restaurant as a dining destination because they assume that the food prices are exorbitant. The ritzy atmosphere may give that impression and keep some people away, but we know better than that. In fact, two people can have a great meal at Il Fiasco for less than $20 – not bad at all. Of course, a few of the menu items are more than $20, but there are plenty of less-expensive alternatives.

You may be a skeptic, thinking that the cheaper menu items are either tiny portions or prison rations – far from the truth. The menu items under $10 are not only substantial portions, but they taste superb. Here's another secret: Between 4 and 6 p.m. and after 9 p.m., every food item on the Bistro Bar menu is half price. You can choose, among other things, southwest calamari, dungeness crab cakes, steamed clams and Cajun coconut prawns for less than $5 each.

Now you are probably thinking that you have to dress formally in order to go there. That won't be necessary. Although some people do dress up, there is no dress code at Il Fiasco, so you may go a little more casual if you like. The atmosphere is on the elegant side, with a little help from the pianist. Il Fiasco also has a reputation for offering a great selection of fine wines; cocktails are available. It's a great place for a business lunch, date or to just treat yourself. Consider making reservations.

Written by Ken Brierly

Restaurants

Dirty Dan Harris'

Address
1211 11th Street
Bellingham WA, 98225

Hours
Every day 5:00pm - 10:00pm

Directions:
Dirty Dans Harris' is across the street from Village Books in
Fairhaven

Features
Full Bar, Takes Reservations, Pool/Billards, Dinner

Description
Dirty Dan Harris' Restaurant is a steak and seafood house located
in Fairhaven. The restaurant takes its name from the founder of
Fairhaven whose Grand Hotel burned down not more then a
block away from the restaurant. Not known for his manners,
Dirty Dan was reputed to be a man of poor personal hygiene
and unpleasant demeanor. It is surprising that one of
Bellingham's finest restaurants is named after one of its most
unkempt characters.

Dirty Dan's is everything that you would expect from a fine
dining establishment, choice cuts of meat, fine seafood, served
with cloth napkins and several sets of silverware. They don't have
fancy sauces nor vegetables you don't know the names of. What
they do have is their specialty, choice cuts of charbroiled prime
rib, New York steaks, and tenderloin. The prime rib is excellent.
Year round they serve salmon, Alaskan lobster and Alaskan king
crab plus seasonal specials.

The close quarters, low lighting levels and a split-level structure
lend to the elegant ambiance. The main level is generally for the
see-and-be-seen while the bottom floor is for more intimate
dining. The top floor has a full bar and a pool table in the back
past the bar. Be aware of the prices: unless you are celebrating
another decade of living or can afford a house in the Edgemoor
area you probably won't be able to dine here very often.

You will need to make reservations ahead of time for Dirty Dan's.
The restaurant opens only for dinner and is usually very busy.
If you have to wait, browsing around historical Fairhaven is a
perfect way to pass the time.

Written by Wayne Berry

Dutch Mothers

Address
405 Front
Lynden WA, 98264

Hours
Mon-Sat 6:00am - 10:00pm

Directions:
Drive into Lynden on Front Street. Dutch Mothers will be about 3/4 of the way down the central business district on the right.

Features
Banquet Facilities, Dinner, Lunch, Wheelchair Accessible, Kid Friendly, Breakfast, Espresso, Take-Out

Description
If you have only one opportunity to eat in Lynden, definitely make it the Dutch Mothers. This restaurant will not only feed you really well, but also give you a taste of Holland with it's charming atmosphere and friendly staff.

When you enter the restaurant you are greeted by friendly wait staff in traditional attire (even wooden shoes) and transported to a Dutch village. The interior of the restaurant resembles a village with each seating area decorated like rooms of a house or even an interior courtyard complete with working fountain and skylight. Photographs of tulips and windmills abound to help set the tone. The rooms come in a variety of sizes and can accommodate small groups and parties to large banquets. Their banquet room can seat 120 people. Kids are welcomed with crayons and their own special menu. Adults can choose from a large selection of breakfast, lunch and dinner items. Pot roast, Chicken, Fish and chips, Sausage and porogies, salads, sandwiches and traditional Dutch lunches are all served. Portions are generous so make sure you bring your appetite. Tuesday evenings is family buffet night. The real treat of this restaurant comes when the main meal is over, which you may just want to skip and go straight to the dessert. The desserts temp you as you enter the restaurant with fresh made pies, pastries and even espresso available for carry out. The deep dish pies use locally grown berries, the cream that is used is REAL and that's what makes the difference. With selections like whipped cheesecake, dish apple pie and Edaleen Ice Cream you can't go wrong.

Make sure you allow a little extra time or adjust your meal schedule earlier or later— you may have to wait as this restaurant is extremely popular with both locals and visitors alike. With the quality service, great atmosphere, good main courses and great desserts it certainly wouldn't be a stretch to proclaim Dutch Mothers the best restaurant in Lynden.

Written by Dave Erickson

Restaurants

Win's Drive-in

Address
1315 12th St.
Bellingham WA, 98225

Hours
Mon-Sat 9:30am - 10:00pm
Sun 10:00am - 10:00pm

Directions:
From I-5 and Old Fairhaven Parkway, turn right on 12th Street.
Win's is a couple blocks down on the right.

Features
Dinner, Lunch

Description
A great deal of the appeal of Fairhaven is the historic buildings
and unique, one-of-a-kind shops and restaurants. There are no
chain stores here, nor are there any fast food places — so
common in other parts of town. However, there is an obvious
need for a quick and convenient locale to get burgers, fries and
shakes, and Win's Drive-in fulfills this niche well.

Win's does not conform to the traditional design of the drive-in
with covered stalls and plexi-glass menus. It is in all other
respects the classic, small-town, independent burger joint. There
are two small windows outside the building for customers to
order from when weather permits. Interestingly enough, one is
solely dedicated to the sale of Lotto and scratch lottery tickets.
It isn't uncommon for a line to form at the window when the
jackpot rises. The interior is exactly what you would expect —
booths lining the wall from the front counter to the back room.
Although there were quite a few paintings of Native American
scenes and Bellingham, past and present, I was most impressed
with the stained-glass representation of a hamburger, shake and
fries by the front door.

One thing is certain: The menu does not disappoint those that
appreciate fast food. Everything that can be deep fried or grilled
is offered, from chili burgers, hamburgers, fishwiches and
chickenwiches, to onion rings and corn dogs. The fact that I
did not try the mysteriously named "yummy burger" haunts me to
this day. A wide selection of milkshakes and malts cements Win's
as an upholder of the traditional Americana cuisine. I personally
recommend the black raspberry shake, made with real fruit and
ice cream. You ain't going to find that at McDonald's now,
are you?

Written by Glen Berry

Boomer's Drive In

Address
310 N Samish Way
Bellingham WA, 98225

Hours
Sun-Thurs 11:00am - 9:00pm
Fri 11:00am - 10:00pm
Sat 11:00am - 10:00pm

Directions:
It's right at the end of Samish Way
where it turns toward downtown.

Features
Dinner, Lunch

Description

There is a reason why Boomer's Drive-in is always busy. It might
be the blast-from-the-past, 50s appeal. It may be the location of a
drive-in on a former cruising strip. However, the safe bet would
have to be the great burgers and shakes that everyone thinks
about as they drive by the restaurant.

Inside the restaurant is a small dining area with a fireplace, which
seems at odds with the mural of a hamburger and splattering
mustard. However, this isn't where most of the food gets eaten.
Boomer's is a true drive-in with the stalls and lighted signs next
to the car windows so patrons can peruse the menu. You turn
your lights on when you're ready to order. No, there aren't mini-
skirt-clad carhops on roller skates but the staff always has some
cute girls. Kids' meals come in cardboard pink Cadillac boxes in
another nod to the 50s feel of the business.

As the flying neon burger in the window indicates, the main business of the place is hamburgers: big hamburgers and good hamburgers. You can get them any way you want, with Swiss, teriyaki,
mushrooms, honey Dijon and a variety of other choices. If you
can't handle the beef try out the veggie, fish and chicken
options. That isn't to say that there are all kinds of fancy, yuppie
treats on the menu, mind you. The rest of the menu is purely
milkshakes and waffle fries, complementing great burgers.

Written by Glen Berry

Restaurants

Pioneer Restaurant

Address
2005 Main St.
Ferndale WA, 98248

Hours
Every day 2:00pm - 1:30am

Directions:
From I-5 take the Ferndale 262 exit. Head west across the Nooksack. the Pioneer will be on your left just past the light at First Avenue.

Features
Pool/Billards, Dinner, Takes Reservations, Beer and Wine, Full Bar

Description
There is nightlife in Ferndale and the Pioneer Restaurant and Lounge has it all. Formerly known as Everybody's Restaurant and Lounge, the Pioneer is located in downtown Ferndale just minutes from I-5.

The pioneer is not your run-of-the-mill restaurant and lounge. With a full menu that features steak, seafood and burgers you can find something to satisfy everyone's taste at reasonable prices. The restaurant is a popular location for large groups and parties. Groups wanting to hold their event at the Pioneer should contact Nellie to reserve space. The staff at the Pioneer is very friendly and helpful. The clientele is also generally friendly, sometimes maybe even a little too friendly if that's possible. The restaurant has a small dance floor and the subdued lighting in the restaurant makes dancing less intimidating. Weekends feature the only live music in town. Because times and acts vary, you should call in advance to find out who is playing. There is good ventilation in the restaurant so non-smokers will probably not be bothered by smoke.

If dancing, live music and food is not what you're after, the Pioneer also features a full service bar, pull tabs, a game room with great pinball machines, pool and darts for your entertainment. Kids are welcome in the Pioneer until 9:00 p.m. after that, it's adults only. Parking on Main Street is limited, but there is additional parking available in a vacant lot on the corner of First Avenue and Main Street.

The Pioneer Restaurant and Lounge is your best choice for an evenings entertainment in Ferndale. The friendly staff, food and drink and variety of entertainment make this restaurant the place to be seen, or not seen.

Written by Dave Erickson

Bob's Burgers & Brew

Address
1304 12th St.
Bellingham WA, 98225

Hours
Mon-Thurs 11:00am - 10:00pm
Sat 11:00am - 11:00pm
Fri 11:00am - 11:00pm
Sun 10:00am - 10:00pm

Directions:
From downtown Bellingham, take State St. out to Fairhaven and stay on it til it turns into 12th St. After the first set of lights, Bob's is in on your right and is clearly marked.

Features
Kid Friendly, Banquet Facilities, Dinner, Lunch, Sunday Brunch, Wheelchair Accessible, Beer and Wine, Full Bar, Smoke-free, Takes Reservations

Description
After a long cross-country drive to begin a new life here in Bellingham, I arrived in Fairhaven practically faint with hunger and thirst. I pulled into the Fairhaven market parking lot with no idea where to go to satisfy my appetite. I then saw the sign across the street: Bob's Burgers and Brew. I was drawn in the door like a moth to firelight. A gourmet burger and a mighty fine brew were just the ticket. That was the first time I went to Bob's.

The atmosphere in Bob's is warm, comfortable, and casual; the staff are friendly, attentive, and make you feel at home. The interior is red brick with wooden tables and chairs and unobtrusive lighting. It is a popular student hangout and yet family friendly.

The menu has an excellent selection of gourmet beef, chicken, and garden burgers with a choice of fries, jojos, potato salad or soup. For those non-burger-oriented types, Caesar salads and house dinners of steak, chicken, or seafood are delicious alternatives. The brew selection is also quite extensive, offering various beers on tap, as well as bottled domestic, imported, popular and local micro brews. I opted to try the Orchard St. Pale Ale. If brew is not your style, Bob's also has a delightful selection of margaritas, daiquiris, frozen cocktails, and ice cream drinks, alcoholic and non-alcoholic alike.

When my well-garnished bacon cheeseburger arrived I had to fight my way through the generous portion of french fries to get to it. The burger was huge, juicy, and cooked medium rare, the way I like it. My advice is to try to eat the burger before downing all the fries or you will be taking it home in a doggy bag. Unfortunately, I had no room left for an ice cream sundae or a piece of pie that are Bob's dessert specialties.

One of the nicest things about Bob's Burgers and Brew is the prices. Meals are fairly inexpensive and the helpings plentiful.

Note: Bob's has a full bar that is separate from the restaurant. It is open every day until 1:00 am and you have to be over 21 to be served. They offer a Sunday breakfast buffet beginning at 10:00 am. There is also a banquet room for special occasions.

Written by Hilary Higgins

Restaurants

Mallard Ice Cream

Address
207 E. Holly St.
Bellingham WA, 98225

Hours
Sun 11:00am - 9:00pm
Mon 11:00am - 10:00pm
Wed 11:00am - 10:00pm
Tues 11:00am - 10:00pm
Thurs-Sat 11:00am - 11:00pm

Directions:
Drive NW on E. Holly. Mallard is on the right hand side through the intersection of Holly and N. State, just before Railroad.

Features
Kid Friendly, Espresso, Wheelchair Accessible, Smoke-free

Description
Have you ever wished you could go for ice cream at a place that was a little out of the ordinary? Ever wanted to keep the kids entertained (even after the ice cream was gone) while you finished your conversation? How about enjoying a homemade milkshake or malt on a college budget?

Mallard Ice Cream is the place for you. Step inside and you'll find brightly painted walls, modern furniture, a small counter with a single register, and beautiful handcrafted flavor tags on the back board, each one vastly different from the others. A miniature multi-colored table against one wall provides the perfect spot for kids; crayons and board games tempt all ages from the shelves. Art hangs on the one brick wall. Community leaflets stashed in the corner remind of the latest local events. And, most likely, you'll only be one of several in line.

All of the ice cream here is homemade. Mallard offers the traditional chocolate, vanilla, and strawberry, as well as some familiar "specialty" flavors, like mint oreo, peanut butter, and chocolate raspberry. But even I was surprised to find chai tea and mocha breve on the menu, enticing me to return in the near future. The ice cream comes in "inner child," small, and medium sizes, and is available in a cone or a dish. For those looking for something a little more adventurous, all ice cream can be made into shakes or malts, or try a brownie sundae or a banana split. Need something to warm you when you're finished? Mallard serves coffee, hot chocolate, hot tea, chai tea, and espresso. Italian sodas and some bottled pop is also available.

Mallard Ice Cream is worth checking out, whether you're looking to discover a new flavor or just a homemade version of your favorite. And look for the mascot: a Mallard duck decoy perched on the partial wall.

Written by Kimberly Baer

Calumet

Address
113 E. Magnolia St.
Bellingham WA, 98225

Hours
Sun-Wed 11:00am - Midnight
Thurs-Sat 11:00am - 1:00am

Directions:
Going down Holly Street, go right on
Railroad Avenue. Go down one block
to Magnolia and then left. The
Calumet is on the right next to
Cellophane Square.

Features
Beer and Wine, Dinner, Dinner, Full
Bar, Lunch, Outdoor seating, Smoke-
free, Takes Reservations, Wheelchair
Accessible

Description
A large, presumably empty, can of Calumet Baking Soda sits inside
the Calumet on a bookcase. I'm not sure if the owners have a
particular affection for Calumet Baking Soda or if it is a source of
pride they use that brand in their restaurant. But it is there, perhaps revealing an answer to the unasked question, "Why do you
call this place the Calumet?"

A long time ago in a galaxy far, far away a waterfront bar stood
where the Calumet now exists; the bar's exterior décor consisted
of wood pilings, rope and fake seagulls. The Calumet is fairly new,
opening in October of '97 and much more aligned with the new,
hip Bellingham than was the bar it replaced.

The menu offers a blend of different styles and tastes, from pastas
and salads to soups and quiches. The Calumet is perhaps better
known for its blended and mixed drinks, which arrive in a variety
of vivid colors.

The Calumet boasts live jazz, which serves as unobtrusive background music while you dine. The walls are decorated with local
art — one artist in front and another in back in a gallery-style display. Rounding out the atmosphere is a moody, possibly romantic
lighting design. Patrons tend to dress a little sharper in accor-
dance with the sophisticated feel of the restaurant.

Written by Glen Berry

Restaurants

La Fiamma

Address
200 East Chestnut
Bellingham WA, 98225

Hours
Every day 11:00am - 11:00pm

Directions:
Head down Railroad to the water past the Seafirst bank and you should see it in the low, brick building right below the Herald.

Features
Dinner, Lunch

Description
In the past ten years, it seems that there has been an emergence of a niche market in restaurants that specialize in fast food, but with a hip, classy twist. La Fiamma is an example of an eatery that has taken pizza upscale in another addition to the downtown restaurant scene.

The restaurant is housed in a renovated brick building like many of the new businesses in the downtown area. The interior has been redone in a post-modern, industrial look, with aluminum flashing and exposed heating vents along the ceilings.

The tables follow suit with a riveted metal design — a contrast to the finished wooden chairs and trim. Large windows make for a bright, cheery atmosphere with a view of the hustle of activity on Railroad Avenue. The menu offers lunch specials, but the restaurant is usually busiest in the evening.

La Fiamma joins the elite of pizzerias by cooking with a wood fired oven — the hallmark of gourmet pizza. Pies come topped with the exotic ingredients you might expect, including prosciutto, cracked pepper, smoked mozzarella, sun-dried tomatoes and assiago cheese. Sauce bases also offer a variety as well, with the classic tomato, onion-garlic or pesto. Although the main focus of the restaurant is pizza, there is an offering of pasta, salads and soups. A few dishes out of the ordinary that might tempt the gourmet are caponata (grilled eggplant), hummus (white bean) and antipasto.

Written by Glen Berry

Community

The Fourth Corner has always been united by a strong sense of community. One need only look at the burgeoning number of diverse organizations and events devoted to educating and assisting the public at large to see that Whatcom County is home to socially aware people.

Whatcom County has the distinction of having twice the national average of family households and that is reflected in its interest in supporting children's events and organizations. Local public schools, museums and children's advocacy groups look out for the needs of the youth of the community with workshops, activities and educational experiences.

Along the same lines, public service organizations and institutions like the Whatcom Literacy Council, Whatcom Community College and Bellingham Technical College offer many services to the community. By educating and offering job skills, they exist to constantly improve the quality of life for area residents.

Citizens are vocal participants in local government, bringing energy and enthusiasm to advisory boards and committees. A politically active community, The Fourth Corner is no stranger to protest and demonstration, whether it be in reaction to local, state or federal policies. Local institutions are not just rubber stamp bureaucracies, but dynamic fixtures serving the needs of the public.

True to Bellingham's cosmopolitan reputation and strong connections outside the region, the city has an impressive array of transportation options available to its citizens. Public transit is alive and well in the local WTA, serving the communities of the entire county. Numerous cities are accessible by ferry, train, bus and via Bellingham's International Airport.

Community

Bellingham City Hall

Address
210 Lottie
Bellingham WA, 98225

Hours
Mon-Fri 8:00am - 5:00pm

Directions:
From Holly Street, turn right on Commercial and drive past
Magnolia, Champion and Flora streets and the public library.
You'll see the flag poles on the left.

Features
Wheelchair Accessible

Description
Flapping Old Glories run up each of the six towering poles lining
the sidewalk outside the main entrance of Bellingham City Hall.
Inside, like cogs in a machine of governance, public employees,
citizens and civic officials bustle from office to office, each conducting the tasks necessary to maintain a civilized and dynamic
community. This center of civic business has a lot going on under
one roof.

Bellingham's City Hall houses most of the city's governing depart-
ments and public services. Among other bureaucratic offices
residing at City Hall, citizens can access the City Council office
and attend City Council meetings and the meetings of other
Bellingham boards and commissions. The Department of Planning
and Community Development can answer zoning and land-use
questions, while planning for and overseeing the city's vision for
growth. Building permits may be applied for at the Building
Services Division. Fines, tickets, business licenses and
water/sewer bills can be paid at the Finance Department office.
Municipal Court and the offices of personnel and the mayor are
also at City Hall.

The two-story marble edifice was constructed in 1939, one of
many projects furthered by the President Roosevelt-sponsored
"New Deal" legislation. Until a few years ago, City Hall was also
home to the Bellingham Police Department. Having badly out-
grown its headquarters, a new BPD station was built down the
block and thus a portion of City Hall was renovated in 1994 to
better use the additional space left by the relocated BPD.

Written by Ken Brierly

Whatcom Courthouse

Address
311 Grand Ave.
7:00am - 5:30pm
Bellingham WA, 98225

Hours
Mon-Fri

Directions:
From Holly Street, turn right on
Flora and go left on Grand Avenue.
It's a couple blocks on the left.

Features
Wheelchair Accessible

Description

A thoroughly modern building, the Whatcom County Courthouse has a contemporary design of clean lines and glass, the lower section being composed of more traditional red brick. The building is particularly impressive at night, lit from below with bright diffused light. Entering the building involves passing through a glass door (with a sign informing visitors that no weapons are allowed in the building) into a foyer under a high, arched dome. Walking up a few marble stairs brings you to the information desk. Apparently there aren't that many people who want to know what is in the courthouse building, because there is no guide to the building or the offices. The nice lady in the council office told me that, aside from the internal phone directories, there is no listing for the building, so I went from floor to floor to read the placards outside of each elevator.

The first floor contains the offices of the Assessor, Auditor, County Executive, County Council, Council Chambers, Human Resources, Information Desk, and Treasurer; Second Floor has the Prosecuting Attorney, Superior Court Department 2 and Commissioner's Office; Third is the County Clerk, Superior Court Department 1 and 3, Public Defender and Assigned Counsel; Fourth Floor houses the District Court Clerk, District Court Probation and District Court Court Rooms; 5th floor is Juvenile Court Services (whose staff cannot offer legal advice, so don't even ask. You should consult your attorney or library resources for assistance), Superior Court, Juvenile Court Room, Administrative Services and Finance/Purchasing. Sixth floor is Juvenile Detention.

There are many closed-circuit cameras unobtrusively planted throughout the building, including inside the elevators. Tasteful, low-maintenance grey carpet graces the floors and creamy pink hollow metal columns line the sterile hallways of all six floors. There is a triple set of plexi-glass doors at the entrance to the Juvenile Detention center. I did not try to enter. There are no weapons allowed here either but there is a nice reminder on the wall in case you missed the one at the entrance. I was looking for a view of the city and I found it on the south end of the fifth floor. Strangely enough, the view from the window not only affords a fantastic view of Bellingham Bay, Lummi Island, the South Hill and the museum, but also the building which houses "A-Quick Bail Bonds" and its red, neon 24hrs sign. *Written by Glen Berry*

Community

Lynden City Hall

Address
323 Front St
Lynden WA, 98264

Directions:
Head down Front Street toward the museum and City Hall is just a few doors before that.

Features
Wheelchair Accessible

Description
On the first floor of Lynden City Hall, under a wall clock and next to a radiator, are two wooden chairs sitting side by side across from the County Clerk's office. If you sit in one of those chairs for a few minutes, City Hall will serve as a reminder of school days, lunch box days, recess and locker days. The staircase is wide. And on the landing there are two tall windows that begin high enough up for a child, a smaller adult even, to need to stand on their tiptoes just to touch the sill.

Just the same, City Hall is an intriguing building. From the street it looks like an odd, but somehow very smooth, combination of Mayberry and a hacienda. On the main floor, past the County Clerk's office, is the Mayor's office. And something about the big wooden door, the textured glass next to it, MAYOR'S OFFICE and a large seal painted on the glass . . . something about that frame is so endearing. And if you climb the stairs to the court room and peer inside, you'll see on the wall directly across from the door, beyond and above the folding tables and the leatherette chairs, a grinning eight by ten of Bill Clinton. It's as if someone painstakingly made an effort at both patriotism and decor in one wall hanging. Or perhaps the idea was that justice must, justice would prevail if only the President himself was smiling down. Either way you find yourself smiling at the warm naivete that makes the cynicism and sourness of the law, of politics, of bureaucracy bearable.

The basement houses no offices, only the restrooms, storage and perhaps cleaning supplies. But there is, thankfully, a bathroom on the main floor. It is clean and sweet smelling, handicap accessible and within earshot of the comforting sounds of doors opening and closing, phones ringing, people walking, talking.

If you sit in a wooden chair underneath the wall clock, go upstairs and look at the grinning Bill, you will find that there's more to City Hall than meets the eye.

Written by Holly Gray

Amtrak

Address
401 Harris Ave
Bellingham WA, 98225

Hours
Every day 8:30am - 11:00am
Every day 5:30pm - 8:00pm

Directions:
On Harris Avenue, go toward the bay. Near the shipyards, the station is about a block before the Ferry terminal on the right.

Features
Wheelchair Accessible

Description
Over the years, the Fairhaven waterfront has evolved into the city's transportation center with the Alaska Ferry, Greyhound Bus Line terminal and Amtrak station conveniently grouped in the same area. The bus and train terminals are cloistered in the same building between Harris Avenue, and, surprisingly enough, the train tracks that run along the bay.

The brick building which houses the two terminals was renovated in 1994 and has a fresh, modern appearance. The wood ceiling, tile floor and large, wooden benches make a pleasant waiting area for departures. Two windows offer information for the respective services of Greyhound and Amtrak. Also, there is everything you would expect, including local bus information, public pay phones and taxi services. Whatcom Transportation Authority buses make three connections per hour at the station; for more information on bus schedules, see the WTA write-up. A small coffee shop called The Fairhaven Station also occupies space in the same building and offers coffee, newspapers and magazines for travelers. Interestingly enough, the South Precinct of the Bellingham Police Department is also a tenant of the building.

Amtrak offers train service on Service 761; the runs between Seattle to Vancouver, British Columbia make stops in Blaine, Bellingham, Mount Vernon and Everett. The north-bound train arrives at 9:52 a.m. and the south-bound train departs at 7:27 p.m. Connections can, of course, be made in Seattle for nationwide destinations.

Written by Glen Berry

Community

Bellingham Airport

Address
4201 Mitchell Way
Bellingham WA, 98225

Hours
Every day 4:00am - 1:00am

Directions:
The exit is well signed off of I-5. It's about ten minutes from the border if you're coming south, or from the north, the exit immediately following the Bellis Fair Mall. Once off I-5, it's your second right, but again, it's well signed.

Features
Bathrooms, Wheelchair Accessible

Description
Bellingham International Airport is the biggest little airport I have ever seen. The airport is a waypoint between the large airfields in Vancouver, British Columbia and Seattle, and it takes the job just as seriously. Alaska and Northwest (working through Horizon Air), and United Express can get you just about anywhere in the world you need to go. On a local level, Harbor Air provides service to the San Juan Islands. West Isle Air does so as well, and also flies to Vancouver, Victoria and other Canadian cities.

If you are to visit the area, Avis, Budget, Hertz and National all operate full-service car rental offices in the terminal and a hotel board provides phone access to most of the area lodgings, as well as shuttle service to and from. Being only thirty minutes from Canada by car and much less by plane, the terminal also features a duty-free shop and customs office.

Bellingham International is also one of the better airports in the area for small plane pilots. They have their own tower and provide local guidance, while external airspace is controlled from Vancouver. They provide fuel, maintenance and ample tie downs for parking. The runway routinely accepts 727s and 737s, and has even taken a DC-10 from time to time.

Speaking of parking, the airport has both short-term and long-term parking facilities, priced at about eighty cents an hour and thirty dollars a week.

Written by Dave Shepherd

Greyhound

Address
401 Harris Ave.
Bellingham WA, 98225

Hours
Mon-Fri 9:00am - 11:00pm
Sat Midnight - 7:00pm

Directions:
On Harris Avenue, go toward the bay. Near the shipyards, the station is about a block before the Ferry terminal on the right.

Features
Bathrooms

Description
Over the years, the Fairhaven waterfront has developed into the transportation center of the city, with the Alaska Ferry, Greyhound terminal and Amtrak Station all gathered in the same area. The bus and train terminals are conveniently cloistered in the same building between Harris and, surprisingly enough, the train tracks along the bay.

Greyhound offers bus service from Seattle to Vancouver on route 601, with stops in Blaine, Mount Vernon and Everett.

The brick building which houses the two terminals was renovated in 1994 and has a clean, modern appearance. The wood ceiling, tile floor and large, wooden benches make for a pleasant waiting area for departures. Two windows offer information for their respective services from Greyhound and Amtrak. There is also everything you would expect, including local bus information, public payphones and taxi services. Be aware that when a train or bus arrives, there is quite a taxi rush, especially in the evening after the WTA buses no longer run. There is a small coffee shop, The Fairhaven Station, which also occupies space in the same building and offers coffee, newspapers and magazines for travelers.

Written by Glen Berry

Community

Cruise Terminal

Address
355 Harris Ave.
Bellingham WA, 98225

Hours
Tues 8:30am - 4:30pm4:30pm
Wed 8:30am -
Thurs 8:30am - 4:30pm
Mon 10:00am - 4:30pm

Directions:
From Old Fairhaven Parkway, turn right on 12th street and left on Harris. The Cruise Terminal in on the right near the end of Harris.

Features
Wheelchair Accessible

Description
More commonly known as the Alaska Ferry Terminal, the Cruise Terminal serves as a host for many different ferry and cruise companies. These public and private companies offer service to Alaska, the San Juan Islands as well as Victoria, BC and whale watching cruises.

The terminal is the southern-most destination for Alaska's Marine Highway System (AMHS). The AMHS (1.800.642.0066) offers year round service from Bellingham to Alaska. The ferry system is equipped to handle both cars and passengers on the 2-3 day trip. There is a covered, heated area of the deck for campers or, for a extra charge, accommodations are available in cabins.

The San Juan Island Commuter offers quick and inexpensive service directly from Bellingham. The ships are passenger only but they do stop at many of the islands that the WSDOT ferries do not, including Sucia, Eliza and Stuart in addition to Lopez, Orcas and San Juan.

Day cruises are also offered direct from Bellingham to Victoria, BC on Vancouver Island. The trip is right around three hours and cost is $74.

Written by Glen Berry

WTA

Address
2011 Young Street Suite 201
Bellingham WA, 98225

Directions:
The bus terminal is right downtown on the east end of Railroad Ave.

Description
Whatcom Transportation Authority forms the core of public transportation, not only for Bellingham, but Whatcom County as well. Buses originate at the bus terminal on Railroad Avenue downtown and serves Bellingham with routes to Ferndale, Lynden and Blaine. WTA also offers specialized transportation for the elderly, people with disabilities and offers vanpools as well.

Bus schedules may be obtained downtown at the WTA terminal or grab a route map from any one of its individual buses. Frequency depends upon area but buses typically run every half-hour for most routes. Generally, most buses pass through the transit terminal on Railroad at the midpoint on their routes. Transfers are not free but considering the low cost of riding, the price for the second fare is not unreasonable. You can call 676-RIDE and get personalized help figuring out which buses you need to take to get from A to B.

Other services by WTA include Dial-A-Ride, where persons can call and make a reservation to have a van pick them up at any location much like a taxi. Eligibility restrictions are minimal, but you should call ahead to determine availability in your area. The cost is the same as a bus fare, 50-cents. WTA also maintains a fleet of vans for carpools, which are leased to commuter groups who pay a fee based on daily travel distance and number of passengers.

Written by Glen Berry

Community

Children's Museum

Address
227 Prospect St.
Bellingham WA, 98225

Hours
Tues, Wed, Sun Midnight - 5:00pm
Thurs-Sat 10:00am - 5:00pm

Directions:
From Holly Street, go right on Prospect at the Holly/Bay street intersection. The museum is just past the main museum.

Features
Kid Friendly

Description
Anyone traveling down Prospect Street would find the Whatcom Children's Museum hard to miss. The side of the building is a mural of bright colors, soft rounded shapes, images of the harbor, ships and the mountains around the bay. The windows are decorated with paper cut-outs in the shape of geometric designs which let light into the inside.

The exterior is indeed a reflection of the nature of the Children's Museum — a place of learning and fun for young children. Hands-on learning is emphasized with interactivity being the key element in the majority of exhibits and exercises. Sensory exhibits which demonstrate the bio-mechanical operation of the senses are a regular feature. A puppet theater occupies one corner of the museum. There are also craft and art workshops in a classroom-type setting. Field trips and "Wonder" workshops are also offered on a regular basis. "Wonder" boxes are also provided — Tupperware tubs with fun, educational material for children to work with to learn on their own. Two computers are also available for use, although I will admit it was a bit odd seeing them on a desk that was just two-feet high.

Aimed at children one- through eight-years old, the museum serves many functions beyond those of traditional historical organizations. The Children's Museum style is half way between a preschool and a hands-on learning organization, such as the Pacific Science Center in Seattle. The museum charges an admission fee of $2 to partially recover costs. Although the museum is operated by the same organization as the Whatcom Museum and receives money through Whatcom Society fundraisers, it is not operated by the city. The museum is popular, visited by a rough average of 80 people per day, but on winter weekends attendance can climb as high as 150.

Written by Glen Berry

Lynden Community Center

Address
401 Grover St.
Lynden WA, 98264

Hours
Mon-Fri 9:00am - 5:00pm
Sat 9:00am - 1:00pm

Directions:
Take the Guide out to Lynden and turn right onto Front St. and follow it into downtown Lynden. Take a left on 5th St. and the Center is on your right, on the corner of 5th and Grover St.

Description
The Lynden Community/Senior Center's motto is "we are in the people business."

A typical day at the center might include: exercise class, the Looney Toon Kitchen band practice, a nutritional lunch, bridge; Bocce Ball; hymn singing or a City Council Meeting, such is the diversity of activities you might find happening at the Lynden Community/Senior Center on any given day.

Located in downtown Lynden, this red brick building was once a grocery store. It was purchased in 1991 with funding from the city, the Lynden Council on Aging, and Whatcom County Parks. It was turned into a multi-purpose facility that provides a wide range of services and recreational activities for Seniors and the Community alike.

During the day, the Center is primarily used by Seniors. If you look up on their schedule board as you enter the building, you will find that each day is packed with activities like the ones shown above. The center has approx. 500-600 members. Lunch is served 6 days a week for approximately 75-80 people. Anyone 60 or over may come for lunch, a donation is recommended. The main room with stage is primarily used for lunches, band practice, organization meetings, and scheduled entertainment. There is also a pool room with four pool tables. I hear from Bob Long, the Center's manager, that ladies pool on Mondays has become quite popular. In addition there is a crafts and exercise room, a TV room/lounge, gift shop, card room for bridge and pinochle, and a health room.

In the evenings, the Center is open for community use such as town council and county meetings. Several local Bellingham businesses meet there regularly, including the Whatcom Transit Authority and Haggen. Various religious denominations have also used the Center for services. As Bob says "almost anything goes." Local groups needing practice, performance, or meeting space should feel free to get in touch with him to obtain more information about scheduling space.

With such a diversity of services and activities, I can safely say that the Lynden Community/Senior Center definitely lives up to its motto.

Written by Hilary Higgins

Community

Church of the Assumption

Address
2116 Cornwall Ave.
Bellingham WA, 98225

Hours
Sun 9:00am - 12:30am
Sat 5:00pm - 6:00pm
Wed 5:00pm - 6:00pm

Directions:
From I-5 Iowa Street exit, drive west to James Street and turn right. Turn left on Kentucky and follow street to Cornwall Avenue. The church is on the right, next to Bellingham High School.

Features
Wheelchair Accessible

Description
Most would agree the Church of the Assumption is one of Bellingham's most striking landmarks, visible from just about anywhere in the city. The building is revered for several reasons. The church's stained-glass windows, depicting various saints, are particularly important and priceless due to the fact that such large and intricate window art are not a commonplace feature of modern churches. Inside, the balcony at the back of the church holds the largest pipe organ north of Seattle. It is not uncommon for visitors to go inside the cavernous building and gaze at the impressive arches, stained glass windows and dark wooden pews which line the church.

The towering steeple of the brick structure has steadfastly speared the city's skyline for nearly 80 years. However, the roots of this Catholic church go back more than 100 years. The original Church of the Assumption was a wooden edifice that overlooked the bay on South State Street. Due to the town's growing population, the church purchased the current property on Dock (Cornwall) Street in the early 1900's. There, a parochial school was built in 1916, but due to World War I, the church was not built until 1920.

A huge iron-cast bell is still perched in the steeple tower, but inconvenience has given way to an electronic chime in recent years. The real bell has been rung only twice in the last 25 years: once to commemorate the end of the Vietnam conflict, and later, marking the church's centennial — a 100-toll stint. Over the years, the church, school and pastoral center have remained largely the same. A large gymnasium on the property is host to the parish's annual fall celebration, Harvest Festival, held during the first full weekend in October and draws thousands of visitors from the community.

Written by Ken Brierly

Dutch Village Inn

Address
655 Front St. # 7
Lynden WA, 98264

Directions:
Drive north on Guide Meridian to Lynden. Turn right on Front Street and follow signs to Dutch Village Mall.

Description
Upon arriving at the Dutch Village Mall, one can't help but notice the 72 foot windmill on its south end, the blades slowly turning far above the window shoppers lingering on the sidewalk. While adding intrigue and beauty to this area of Lynden, the windmill also houses three of the six rooms available at the Dutch Village Inn. The Inn's mall location allows its guests easy access to gift shops, miniature golf, Queen Juliana Theatre, and the Sidewalk Café, all within walking distance of the rooms.

Each room is unique in its décor and layout, and subsequently has its own unique Dutch name. Room prices vary due to number of beds and additional luxuries, such as a hot tub or an extra bathroom. However, all room prices include a complimentary Dutch style breakfast. Prices can also be reduced with rental of the entire hotel or single occupancy in any room. Reservations require a non-refundable deposit, and the Inn requests that cancellations be made three days prior to the reserved date. Pets are not allowed, so leave Rover at home, and smoking is in designated areas only. For motor home travelers, the Inn has seven RV spaces available, all with full hook-up. Call or write to the Inn for reservations or more information.

Written by Kimberly Baer

Community

Fairhaven Public Library

Address
1117 12th Street
Bellingham WA, 98225

Hours
Mon-Sat 1:00pm - 6:00pm

Directions:
West on Fairhaven Parkway. Right on 12th. 3 Blocks to the library.

Features
Wheelchair Accessible, Kid Friendly

Description
A truer community library could not be found. While the downtown Library is a megalith with all sorts of research facilities; the Fairhaven branch, while in every respect a true library, is really a haven for the readers amongst us. In 1890 a small group of people began the Fairhaven Reading Room in the Mason Building so men could 'spend a evening somewhere besides a saloon.' A child who grew up in Fairhaven could climb 3 flights of stairs to get a book; so in 1904 a new library was built. Andrew Carnegie promised $12,500, and the construction was begun. (He also promised some funds to begin a northern library because it was so difficult to travel between the two.) The same year he gave an additional $3,500 so the building could be opened that year. It was originally built of red brick on a concrete foundation. (The original brick can be seen at the rear of the building.) In 1974 the interior was remodeled and much of the woodwork was lost. Due to the diligence of the current librarian and the Fairhaven Friends of the Library the woodwork is being restored and much of the original furniture is being replaced. The imposing building can be credited to Carnegie.

The children's section, originally housed in the basement, boasts its' own iMac, with educational programs fit for adults. (Children have priority. It's their computer.) There is a wide array, and after a choice has been made, you are asked to insert a CD and be taken away. To Africa, Sim City, Swamp Gas Europe! And learn something while you're there. The tables are there from the original library, and hours can be spent there looking through their large selection of children's books.

Meeting Rooms are available for dances, lectures, classes, club meetings and political events. They vary in size and location. The rates are very modest for an hourly rental.

The Adult section, as well as having a large collection of books, old and new, also has Video tapes, Books on Tape, Magazines, CD's a copy machine, and lots of good company.

The atmosphere is very informal, and everyone knows everyone. The service is definitely very personal. A trip to Fairhaven is not complete without a stop here.

Written by Shelagh Considine

Bellingham Public Library

Address
210 Central Ave.
Bellingham WA, 98225

Hours
Mon-Thurs 10:00am - 9:00pm
Fri 10:00am - 6:00pm
Sat 10:00am - 6:00pm

Directions:
From Holly Street, go toward the museum at Bay Street and then left on Central Ave. It's a block down on the left.

Features
Wheelchair Accessible

Description
Located downtown near City Hall and the County Courthouse, the Bellingham Public Library serves Whatcom County as its largest public library. The building is modern, as it was recently renovated. By the numbers, the library holds over 258,000 books in its collection and has a circulation of nearly one million books annually. The library also has a large children's library and a meeting room for local community groups.

As one would expect, the library contains the staples of public libraries: atlases, almanacs, regional phone books, administrative code, Whatcom County Code and Revised Code of Washington. Also available is an entire collection of genealogy, historical registries and local history for research. The collection of magazines is quite respectable; the major newspapers are represented, including all of the periodicals from Washington state. Also, several thousand books may be checked out on tape and a surprisingly wide selection of music CDs are available.

The system for searching for books and periodicals is by computer. Although the system is relatively dated, it is straightforward and easy to use. Searching can be performed by subject, title or author, and all three methods yielded accurate results. The database includes a listing of local community groups and a database of The Bellingham Herald's of past articles, including article dates and abstracts.

Written by Glen Berry

Community

Lynden Public Library

Address
205 4th
Lynden WA, 98264

Hours
Mon-Thurs 10:00am - 9:00pm
Fri 10:00am - 6:00pm

Directions:
Heading north on Guide Meridian, turn left onto Front
Street. Continue on Front St. until 17th Street, then turn left.
Go one block to Grover and turn right. Continue on Grover
until 4th. The Library will be on the northwest
corner of the intersection of Grover and 4th.

Features
Kid Friendly

Description
Walking into Lynden's Public Library revives memories of
the libraries of one's childhood - smallish, cozy, quiet, but
with a low murmur of activity. The Lynden Public Library
occupies a small, single story building just a block or so
from the main Front Street shopping district, so it's a pleasant walk from either a residential or downtown area. The
library has an excellent children's section, cheerfully decorated with construction paper cutouts and bright pictures
and occupying close to a third of the total floor space. The
library also offers many of the things we would expect at a
much larger library: seven computers available for catalog
database searches, one computer for free internet use,
videos, tapes, a good periodicals section, seasonal activities,
outreach services for the homebound, and a book endow-
ment program. And books, of course, lots and lots of books,
including large print books, books on tape, and books in
Spanish.

For almost as long as the town has been in existence,
Lynden has had a public library. The first library was founded by a women's group, and that library eventually was
located in City Hall. The name of the first librarian is
unknown but Mattie Anderson is remembered as a librarian
who, for many years, helped children find their favorite
books - books like Tom Swift, The Rover Boys and The
Bobbsey Twins. In the early 1970's, the library moved to its
present location on 4th Street. Today, the Lynden Library is
part of the Whatcom County Library System, made up of
nine libraries and a bookmobile.

The Lynden Public Library has a much-needed new library
building in its future. The new building will be at least three
times larger than the present site. Current plans include
moving the County's reference center to the new building.

The reference center, currently located in Bellingham, will offer a broad range of high quality reference material and will be more accessible to the public than at its present location. For a family-oriented community, a library having the features of the Lynden Public Library and within walking distance to many neighborhoods, is valuable indeed.

Written by Tanya Perkins

Whatcom Community College

Address
237 W. Kellogg Rd.
Bellingham WA, 98226

Hours
Mon-Fri 7:00am - 10:00pm

Directions:
Take Meridian past Bellis Fair and Bakerview Road. Turn west on Kellogg Road at the intersection with Seafirst Bank. WCC is the complex of buildings beyond the first intersection.

Description
As the population of Bellingham began to explode in the mid-1980s, so did the need for expanded higher education. Today, with Western Washington University beginning to reach its enrollment capacity, Whatcom Community College is becoming more important and popular. Located behind the bustle of Bellis Fair Mall and the Guide Meridian, WCC is gradually expanding its size and options for students and the community.

In recent years, WCC has erected two new educational buildings and a pavilion/gymnasium. Heiner Center, a library and study area, was built a couple years back to meet the demands of a growing student body and community. More recently, Kelly Hall was built and the old library was remodeled to accommodate more classrooms. The majority of the school's buildings are constructed with attractive, dark red bricks. A gymnasium, called the Pavilion, was also constructed to host community and school events. The WCC men's and women's basketball teams — the Orcas — play their home games there and Gov. Gary Locke spoke to the community at a Pavilion reception during fall of 1998.

Community

**Whatcom
Community
College
(continued)**

About 3,500 students are enrolled at WCC, taking classes ranging from English and math to golf and anthropology. Tuition costs are dependent on the number of credits students are enrolled for, but WCC is not only for young adults. The college has a variety of returning student courses and also offers classes for the community which are not for credit: cooking classes, computer classes, photography and foreign language classes, among others. WCC offers credit and non-credit classes during fall, winter, spring and summer quarters.

Written by Tyler Watson

Night Life

Although the term "night life" is normally associated with urban areas and the bright lights of the big city, Bellingham and Whatcom County has its fair share of places to congregate after dark.

Local bars cater to a number of different tastes, from classic working-class taverns to the college bars that line State Street. You'll find no lack of spots for beer drinking, music enjoyment, pinball playing, pool shooting and dart throwing in the city.

Of course, to appeal to more sophisticated palates, Bellingham also has an assortment of establishments specializing in high-quality brews, compelling foods and tasteful atmospheres. These are the brightly lit - and often smoke-free - places you might find the suit-and-tie crowd conducting after-hours business and sharp, young couples winding down from the 9-to-5 grind.

No matter if college classes are in session or not, some parts of downtown Bellingham are more crowded at night than during the middle of the day. With the recent additions of new night clubs, the choice for places to dance has been bolstered: Some styles include break, swing, pogo and freestyle dancing, and hip-hop, rock 'n' roll, techno and R&B among the music choices.

Some local clubs have even revamped and expanded their dance floors and regularly book professional DJs to spin industrial and cutting-edge beats. No matter the tricks you have in your dance repertoire, you'll find the right place to show them off.

Night Life

Bradley's Bordertown Tavern

Address
481 Peace Portal Dr.
Blaine WA, 98230

Hours
Every day 11:00am - 2:00am

Directions:
From I-5 north take exit 276 and cross under the freeway. The
Bordertown Tavern will be on your right about one block down.

Features
Pool/Billards, Pull Tabs, Darts, Over 21

Description
The Bordertown Tavern is the epitome of the typical small town
corner tavern. Located just off of I-5 exit 276 (that's the last exit
before you cross into Canada or the first exit in the United states)
on Peace Portal Drive, the Bordertown is a convenient stop to or
from Canada or to get some quick refreshment while vising some
of Blaine's many downtown shops.

The Bordertown is not your typical dark, seedy tavern. On the
contrary, it is very clean and light with a great southern exposure. Views of the bay make sipping libations even more enjoyable and the sunsets will knock your socks off. The tavern, also
known as Bradley's, features a wide variety of beer and snacks to
munch on. On cloudy days, you can watch sporting events on the
big screen TV, or play darts, and pool or try your luck at pull tabs.
Darts seems to be a favorite of patrons, so you may need to get in
line. The tavern boasts some of the friendliest staff in town.
Clientele however seems to vary from the touristy afternoon
crowd to the "don't sit in my seat" regulars in the evenings. Non-
smokers my find the smoke smell a little difficult to take, even
with the front door open on sunny and warm days. An added
bonus of this tavern is that if you've forgotten to bring a designated driver, the Blaine train station is located behind the tavern for
convenient railroad access.

If you decide to make a run for the border, make it the
Bordertown Tavern. It's the tavern with the American and
Canadian flags outside and the friendly atmosphere inside.

Written by Dave Erickson

Up & Up

Address
1234 N State St.
Bellingham WA, 98225

Hours
Every day 3:00pm - 1:00am

Directions:
Driving down Holly Street, go left on State Street. It is located half-a-block up on the left.

Features
Beer and Wine, Darts, Over 21, Pool/Billards

Description
Longevity can be an indicator of a good business — after all, to stay open requires a working formula for success. The World Famous Up & Up tavern on State Street has been doing it right for more than 15 years. Their key to success: cheap beer, casual atmosphere, entertainment, ample seating and cheap beer.

It may sound too good to be true, but it's too expensive to stay home Wednesday nights: The Up serves up cold pitchers of brew for $1 each. With no cover charge and a pocket full of quarters, a patron can enjoy traditional pub mainstays such as pool (six tables) and electronic darts for no more than five bucks.

For those who choose to ramble among pals, this alehouse has plenty of indoor and outdoor seating. Also, the Up & Up occasionally hosts Celtic-style bands and poetry slams.

For those who would drink a carton of expired milk before consuming Busch or Schmidt, these purveyors of beer also offer local microbrews and standard national brands. Before the stagger home, soak up the stomach suds with a made-to-order hamburger — only $2. A penny-pincher's Utopia, it may go with out saying that the Up is a popular destination for students and anyone else stretching their funds. If a change of scenery is in order, several other drinking establishments are literally a stone's throw away.

All told, if the smoke doesn't bother you and the Doublewide's too packed — or bar-hopping is just getting old altogether — you might find refuge at the Up & Up.

Written by Ken Brierly

Night Life

Village Inn Pub

Address
3020 Northwest Ave.
Bellingham WA, 98225

Hours
Every day 7:00am - 2:00am

Directions:
From the I-5 Northwest Avenue exit, drive south on Northwest
Avenue through two stoplights. The Village is located in the busi-
ness center on the left, across from Yeagers Sporting Goods.

Features
Beer and Wine, Breakfast, Darts, Dinner, Full Bar, Lunch,
Pool/Billards, Pull Tabs

Description
Try to find a reason not to go to The Village. You can't, because
you'll find a little bit of everything at the Village Inn Pub &
Eatery. They have a huge menu with great food the whole family
will enjoy. Need another reason? They have pool tables, video
games and a huge pull-tab bar for gamers to tear into while
sippin' down a stiff drink. Want more? They have a full bar and
television sets. Still need a reason? They book live entertainment
during some nights of the week.

It is impossible to get bored with a place that provides so much
entertainment under a single roof. Food choices include everything from soups, salads, burgers and sandwiches to chicken,
steak, seafood and pasta dinners. The Village is open for breakfast
at 7 a.m. everyday. They offer a children's menu, and kids eat free
on Thursday evenings.

The Village also has a decent selection of microbrews, domestic
beers, wine and, of course, cocktails. Consider convincing the
group to make a stop at The Village during a friends' birthday
celebration. Or plan ahead a little and let them cater your event.
If you're looking for a live show, check Kulshan.com or give
The Village a call to see who's playing. They usually have a good
cover band or country band.

Written by Ken Brierly

3B

Address
1226 N. State St.
Bellingham WA, 98225

Hours
Mon-Fri 2:00pm - 2:00am
Sat 5:00pm - 2:00am

Directions:
From Lakeway, take Holly Street to
State and turn left. The 3B is on the
left mid block, past the YMCA.

Features
Beer and Wine, Full Bar, Over 21,
Pool/Billards

Description

The 3B tavern is one of the few bars around that still book live
shows. Therefore, it's not surprising that owner Aaron Roeder is
largely responsible for the fact that Bellingham still has a music
scene. The 3B is frequently graced with nationally recognized talent which vary in style and background; it also hosts area bands
several times per month, and cover charges, if any, are usually
minimal. To find out who may be playing the 3B, check out
Kulshan.com, give them a call or keep an eye out for the fluores-
cent flyers they post around town. Fridays and Saturdays are usually reserved for local and touring bands and have expanded the
focus to include just about every new genre.

"Trailer park trash" was the prevailing theme when the 3B went
on hiatus for a year and assumed the pseudonym "Doublewide."
No one really ever got used to that name anyway, so as of mid-
February, it changed back to the good old 3B. Other nights of the
week have taken on a DJ and an agenda with a theme. (i.e. "funk
night," and "80s night") The joint has a two-tiered dance floor and
is usually packed with college kids on the theme nights. Beer
choices range from Schmidt in a can and Lucky Lager in a bottle
to micro favorites Haystack Black and Red Hook on tap.

The best thing about the 3B is that, well, it's just cool. Roeder
describes it as "a dive bar," but really, the place has class that transcends its dive bar counterparts. The aesthetics: garage sale-style
ceramic ashtrays, tiger-striped upholstered booths, an elk trophy
mounted on the wall from neck to nose, brightly colored record
albums dangling on strings from the ceiling, a freshly painted
orange wall adorned with framed concert posters, old memorabilia of cheap beer — Hamm's, Pabst, Blatz. Oh yeah — it also has
pool tables and pinball.

Written by Ken Brierly

Night Life

U-Name-It Tavern

Address
312 West Front Street
Lynden WA, 98264

Hours
Sat 11:00am - Midnight
Mon-Fri 10:30am - 1:00am

Directions:
Driving into Lynden from the west, drive almost through the main business district. The U-Name-It will be on your left, almost through town.

Features
Darts, Pool/Billards, Over 21

Description
The "U-Name-It Tavern" in downtown Lynden is appropriately titled. If you can name it, you can find it there.

The U-Name-It has a rustic old time feel from its exterior and is generally nondescript inside. It is a clean establishment with a very large bar and plenty of table seating which can be put together for large gatherings. The menu features a good selection of appetizers ranging from buffalo wings to their Jalapeno Poppers. For those who want something a little more substantial, the tavern also features a number of entrée items ranging from corn dogs and sandwiches to fish and chips, chicken strips and steaks. There is plenty of parking in a city lot right next door if the on street parking is full. The tavern does smell heavily of smoke and you'll even notice it if you are lingering in the entry-way or bench out front so if you are smoke sensitive, you may want to think twice about entering. For the game enthusiasts, the U-Name-It features pool tables with very little waiting, dart boards and a big screen television which usually shows a variety of sporting events. The tavern features a good selection of domestic beers and even a good selection of non-alcoholic drinks for those designated drivers.

The U-Name-It Tavern is far and away the best tavern located in downtown Lynden. This could be because of its good selection of food and drinks, its activities like pool and darts, or its size making it perfect for large group functions. It could also be because the U-Name-It Tavern is the only tavern located in downtown Lynden!

Written by Dave Erickson

Anna's Kaddyshack

Address
1114 Harris St.
Bellingham WA, 98225

Hours
Every day 4:00pm - 2:00am

Directions:
From I-5 and Old Fairhaven Parkway turn right on 12th Street and left at Harris. It's a block down.

Features
Banquet Facilities, Beer and Wine, Dinner

Description
Saunter down Harris Street and you're sure to catch a whiff of hickory smoked barbecue as you pass by Anna's Kaddyshack. Step on in before 9 p.m. and you'll find a smokeless, wheelchair accessible family restaurant, specializing in Southern cuisine.

For starters: Cajun-style barbecued shrimp, homemade fries, beer-battered deep fried onion rings, Texas toothpicks, deep-fried hush puppies and Southern breaded fried okra. Anna's famous hickory smoked barbecue baste, Alaskan king salmon and New York steak from the grill, pasta specials, crab cakes, and an assortment of burger sandwiches guarantee to satisfy food cravings while diners relax in the warm, casual atmosphere, and Anna's is known for its weekly specials.

Swing by after 9 p.m. and it's party time! The dining room walls open up to reveal the stage for the evening's entertainment: Monday and Tuesday is sports night; three huge screens televise the biggest sports events, and the game room (open during all business hours for adults over 21) offers two pool tables and a golf video arcade. Hop on the dance floor Wednesday through Saturday after 9 p.m. to the beat of dancing rock 'n' roll and rhythm and blues.

The flavor, flair and casual atmosphere attributes itself to proprietor Anna Williams, who opened her Kaddyshack's doors on Saint Patrick's Day, 1997. Active in civic affairs, the Whatcom Women in Business awarded Williams the 1995 Professional Woman of the Year honor; she has contributed to the community for the past 14 years.

Anna's Kaddyshack has a banquet room for private parties and is also available for club meetings and socials.

Written by Beth Marsau

Night Life

Harry O's

Address
714 Lakeway Dr.
Bellingham WA, 98226

Hours
Every day 6:00am - 2:00am

Directions:
On Lakeway, turn right immediately east of the freeway overpass.
Next to Fred Meyer.

Features
Banquet Facilities, Beer and Wine, Catering, Dinner, Full Bar,
Wheelchair Accessible

Description
As far as cocktail lounges go, Harry O's may be Bellingham's best
kept secret — but it shouldn't be that way. Those who have
never stepped foot in the place are missing out on yet another
viable destination to get a drink, eat dinner, watch the game and
listen to live music. Located inside the Best Western Lakeway Inn,
Harry O's is one of those places where one knows he or she can
escape from the ordinary nightspots — and the same people that
go them. It's big enough to (usually) have open tables, small
enough to keep a comfortable atmosphere and if you like, spread
out enough to preserve one's anonymity and privacy.

The place is ideal because — and I know this sounds corny —
it's totally cozy. It's difficult to make general statements on the
ideals of a place, but Harry O's truly fulfills a list of "ideals." Here
we go. Harry O's is ideal for business meals and dinner dates
because of the privacy factor. It is an ideal place to stop with a
"significant other" near the conclusion of a night out, due to the
fireplace, subtly and (surprise) privacy. Ideal because it is a low-
key alternative to the mayhem and testosterone of sports bars
during the Big Game. Ideal to see an assortment of bands during
various nights throughout the month. Ideal for congregating
friends during those occasions when it isn't known how many
will show; at Harry O's, groups may add smaller tables to the
main group of tables to ensure inclusiveness.

Check out the dinner specials at Harry O's. A certified chef oper-
ates the kitchen and the specials typically are unordinary yet
mouthwatering. For those large events, full-service catering is
available. Those who have ever been to Harry O's New Year's
bash know what they are all about. Political banquets and fund-
raisers are sometimes hosted there, and Johnny Cash even threw
a shindig at Harry O's some years ago. So check it out — it will
probably prove to be a welcome change of scenery.

Written by Ken Brierly

Downtown Johnny's

Address
1408 Cornwall Ave.
Bellingham WA, 98225

Hours
Mon-Fri 11:00am - 2:00am
Sat 5:00pm - 2:00am
Sun 5:00pm - 2:00am

Directions:
Traveling down Holly Street, turn right on Cornwall Avenue. Downtown Johnny's is a block-and-a-half down the street on the right-hand side.

Features
Beer and Wine, Breakfast, Dinner, Full Bar, Lunch

Description
Downtown Johnny's Restaurant & Nightclub is one of the few downtown locations where clubbers can dance into the early morning while drinking at a full bar. The music is usually hip-hop and the DJ takes requests. The establishment is split into two halves —- one side is the club, the other is the restaurant. The club has a lot of seating — both tables and the bar. In addition, an elevated seating area looks down on the dance floor.

Bar hoppers know that standing in line for a drink is a real downer. This won't happen at Downtown Johnny's because they have cocktail servers who are committed to keeping a full drink in front of you by doing all the leg work. If dancing isn't your gig, check out all the other grinders bust some moves while trying to get their groove on. Every type imaginable comes to Johnny's: businessmen, college students and wanna-be gangsters. The place is dimly lit minus the lighting effects of the dance floor.

Better known as a nightclub, Downtown Johnny's is a good place to get a bite to eat. Serving until 7 p.m., menu choices range from soups, salads and sandwiches to mouth-watering chicken, steak and seafood dinners. For those who like to occasionally sleep in, Downtown Johnny's serves some breakfast items until 4 p.m. Appetizers, pasta and a children's menu are also available.

Written by Ken Brierly

Night Life

Wild Buffalo

Address
208 W. Holly
Bellingham WA, 98225

Hours
Fri 7:00pm - 1:00am
Sat 7:00pm - 1:00am

Directions:
Across Holly from Bellingham
Hardware.

Features
Over 21, Pool/Billards

Description
There is a Dance Club, here in town, that offers the best of the local music scene, with national acts, in a smoke free environment! This is a place you can enjoy brewery beer, on tap or in the bottle, and local wines. It is located at 208 W. Holly St., right across from Bellingham Hardware. Their mission is to start the music early, so they begin at 7pm to 1am. You must be 21 to enjoy the sounds. It is a tavern.

On Fridays, Wild Buffalo will be booking rock, world beat, funk, reggae, etc. Saturday will be dedicated to the blues, blue blues and more blues. On special Thursdays and Sundays they will bring in National and Regional acts. Those will be advertised as special nights.

They ask for your feedback in what you would like to hear, or drink or even nibble at this new club. The physical plant is as exciting as the music planned. I understand a couple of local fellows did the work. They did a great job! When you explore the upstairs billiard room and notice the fine view of the dance floor and the band below, enjoy the copper pipe used as railings. The restrooms rate their own mention. If you encounter that alarm on the backdoor, it really does work! All these amenities are in a smoke-free environment.

Watch for their featured band and cover charge. Give them your feedback. It's your club, too. Enjoy! Call 752-0720 for more information.

Written by Shelagh Considine

Royal

Address
208 E. Holly St.
Bellingham WA, 98225

Hours
Mon-Fri 4:30pm - 1:30am
Sat 4:30pm - 1:30am

Directions:
The Royal is located on Holly Street, between State Street and Railroad Avenue and is open from 4:30 p.m. until 1;30 a.m. Monday through Saturday.

Features
Darts, Over 21, Pool/Billards, Beer and Wine, Dinner, Full Bar, Karaoke, Pool/Billards

Description
The Royal has something for everyone: It's a dance club, a bar, a pool hall and a diner. It is a favorite destination for those looking to have some good times with good drinks. First, it's the largest club in Bellingham, square-footage wise. The Royal features full bars upstairs and downstairs, and each floor has its own agenda. The downstairs part of the establishment has two halves. One half is well lit with huge booths for those who want to drink, eat, chat or all three.

The other side is the dance floor and dark lounge. This is where the live entertainment or DJ and the dance floor is located. Next to the bar is a darkened seating area for those not drunk enough to dance yet. You may order at the bar, but The Royal also has cocktail servers and bussers — always a nice touch. If line dancing or hip-hop is the theme downstairs on a particular night, and that's not your gig, you can get a change of scene upstairs. There you'll find six pool tables, darts, pinball, seating, lighting, a jukebox and the other bar.

The Royal has nightly drink specials and a variety of beers on draught and bottled. Some nights, The Royal charges a minimal cover, but the place is usually hoppin'. Beware of the Long Island iced tea. It has a tendency to sneak up on you, as it is both extremely tasty and potent.

Written by Ken Brierly

Night Life

Factory

Address
1212 N. State St.
Bellingham WA, 98225

Hours
Mon-Fri 6:00pm - 2:00am
Sat 6:00pm - 2:00am

Directions:
From Lakeway, take Holly Street and turn left on State. It is near the end of the block on the left.

Features
Beer and Wine, Over 21

Description
One of Bellingham's newest nightclubs, The Factory is also one of the hippest. The decorative post-modern industrial theme lends The Factory a big-city flair that transcends its local nightclub counterparts. Metallic furniture, industrial equipment parts, and steel fixtures are some of the aesthetics that distinguish the industrial appeal of The Factory. A disco ball above the dance floor and trick lighting, combined with the up-tempo disco/industrial music complete the effect of The Factory.

The Factory serves beer and wine, bottled and draught, and usually has a beer special. Beer choices range from local and regional micros to the standard national macros. Most nights of the week, The Factory features a D.J. who kicks out the latest, hottest jams to keep the dance floor groovin'. For those Factory-goers who take a few more beers before they have the courage to busta move, the place has table, booth and bar seating. In addition, the restrooms are nicer and typically cleaner than your average downtown clubs'. The work of local artists graces The Factory's walls, and owner Reece DeGolier keeps it fresh, frequently rotating the displays.

The Factory's clientele is primarily twenty-somethings and college students. The place is pretty nice and some patrons dress up a little more than you might find at other local bars, but dress is not exclusive — you will see all kinds at The Factory.

Written by Ken Brierly

Rumors Cabaret

Address
1119 Railroad Ave.
Bellingham WA, 98225

Hours
Every day 2:00pm - 2:00am

Directions:
From Lakeway, take Holly Street downtown to Railroad and go left. It's two blocks down on the right.

Features
Beer and Wine, Over 21, Pool/Billards, Pull Tabs

Description
While chain smoking Camel Lights, Owner Wayne Miller makes adamantly clear that, despite some misconception, the new Rumors Cabaret isn't a gay bar. "It's a melting pot. It really has people of all ages from all walks of life," Miller said.

A couple years ago, Rumors moved from its dark, claustrophobic dance club on State Street, to a much larger, sophisticated-looking establishment and dance hall in the 1100 block of Railroad Avenue near the Boundary Bay Brewery. "Back when I bought the business, clubs were dark and dingy," he said.

Miller's decision to move was primarily based on demand reasons. Complications with the landlord at the club's State Street location made expansion there improbable.

The new location is adorned with windows, skylights, high ceilings and modern furnishings — including pinball, pull-tabs and pool tables. Remaining is the steadfast, psychedelic light show on the dance floor side. "Originally, I thought this spot might be too big," Miller says of the warehouse-turned-alehouse. "But it turns out on Friday and Saturday nights, we can have zero dance floor."

A sign hangs outside the front door that alerts the unwitting patron before he or she enters. Stamping out his cigarette, Miller paraphrases: "The sign says anybody's welcome, just keep the attitude out. If you don't understand or tolerate gays or bisexuals (laughs), then it's the wrong place to come to."

A big city look; nice clean area; lots of parking — his buzz words.

He fires up a Camel Light.

Written by Ken Brierly

Night Life

Boundary Bay Brewery

Address
1107 Railroad Ave.
Bellingham WA, 98225

Hours
Mon-Fri 11:00am - 11:00pm
Sat-Sun 9:00am - 11:00pm

Directions:
Driving down Holly Street, turn left on Railroad. It's down two blocks on the right.

Features
Beer and Wine, Lunch, Smoke-free, Wheelchair Accessible

Description
Situated on Railroad Avenue, only blocks away from the water, the Boundary Bay Brewery provides a unique atmosphere for meeting friends and having dinner. Unlike some watering holes in town, Boundary Bay has a bright atmosphere and immediate personality. The high, white vaulted ceiling, adorned with large boat sails, makes the already spacious bar area look even larger. The soft sound of jazz that aerates from the rectangle ceiling-mounted speakers mingles with the conversation and laughter of beer drinkers and diners alike. The dark, hardwood floors contrast with glossy wooden table tops that are sprinkled throughout the lounge. Soft, white Christmas lights hang from bare branches of wiry plants that peer out from the corners of the room. Boundary Bay's wooden architecture is matched in prominence only by its prevailing nautical theme. A series of colorful, massive paintings hang from the white-washed walls.

The Boundary Bay Brewery boasts a variety of beers and wine, including a series of ales crafted in-house. Boundary's Best Bitter, Scotch Ale and Amber are among their specialty selections. Boundary Bay received awards for their Best Bitter and Old Boulder brews at the Boulder, Colo. Great American Beer Festival in 1998.

Separate from the lounge is a restaurant area. Large table lamps illuminate the tables where diners order dishes like cedar plank salmon, seven chili ale-chiladas and the American staple: spaghetti and meatballs. Appetizers, sandwiches, pizzas and black bean humus are other popular dishes.

On occasion, Boundary Bay Brewery hosts live music and other events. On any given night, college students and young people mingle with the middle-aged professional type. Boundary Bay's smoke-free environment can be refreshing to those wishing to escape the sometimes lung punishing bar scene.

Written by Tyler Watson

Orchard Street Brewery

Address
709 W. Orchard Drive
Bellingham WA, 98225

Hours
Mon-Fri 11:30am - 10:00pm
Sat 4:00pm - 11:00pm

Directions:
From the I-5 Guide Meridian exit, drive south on Meridian by the Bellingham Golf and Country Club. Turn on Orchard Street and look for a sign a few hundred yards down on the right. It can be easy to miss.

Features
Beer and Wine, Dinner, Lunch, Smoke-free, Takes Reservations

Description
Size isn't everything. Case-in-point: Orchard Street Brewery is a small restaurant. The menu is short and simple. Only four beers are available on tap. However, being small has its advantages, in that it affords a place to specialize in doing a few things very well. Specialization has helped Orchard Street Brewery thrive.

OSB isn't a destination for rowdy drunks — this place has class. It is a great destination for a date or quiet lunch. It's compact yet comfortable and smoking is not allowed. A friendly wait staff takes orders for such delicious items as sandwiches, salads, pastas and wood-fired pizzas. Diners can watch cooks throw pizzas in the oven or check out the huge brew kettles at work in the next room.

However, the best reason to visit OSB is for the beer. The Rye Ale, Christina Porter, Pale Ale and Stock Ale — brewed on the premises — proves that the best beer is made in small batches. These complex, full-flavored beers are so hearty that they are almost a meal in themselves. Watch out, friends. These are high-octane potions, having an extremely high alcohol content and are catching on in popularity. OSB has expanded its operation in recent months to keep up with retail demand. Washingtonians put away the most micro brews in the country, and Orchard Street Brewery is doing its part to keep Washington state the largest producer of craft beers. If your companion isn't a micro brew aficionado, wine and other beers in the bottle are available.

Written by Ken Brierly

Night Life

Archer Ale House

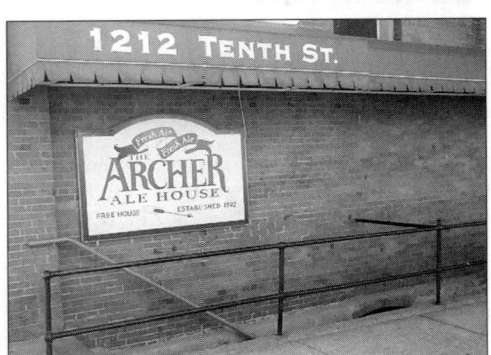

Address
1212 10th St.
Bellingham WA, 98225

Hours
Sun 3:00pm - 9:00pm
Mon-Thurs 3:00pm - 11:00pm
Fri 3:00pm - Midnight
Sat 1:00pm - Midnight

Directions:
From I-5 Fairhaven Parkway exit, drive west to 12th street and turn right. Take a left at Harris Avenue and go right at 10th. Archer's is on the left.

Features
Darts, Beer and Wine, Smoke-free

Description
These days, anyplace that serves a drink can be mislabeled a "bar;" but the bar is the first thing you notice. Archer Ale House is a bar in the traditional sense: A long, dark-stained wooden bar stretches almost the entire length of the main lounge area. The dark wood contrasts with the gold bars and trim that is generously spread through the bar. Holding the massive bar back from spilling out onto the streets of Fairhaven is what could be the most original brick walls in town. The large, bumpy-gray bricks appear to have been built with the idea of holding off an attacking army. Vivid green trim lines the top of the walls that eventually collide with the low, beige ceiling. Authentic English and Celtic music is playing softly through the bar area, giving the extremely clean Archer Ale House a relaxing and warm sense of style.

Sitting at one of the wood tables spread over the multi-shaded green carpet, your mind begins to play tricks on you, and you feel like you're drinking back in England circa 1900. Beer menus at the tables list a variety of local and import beers. A rating scale helps drinkers to choose a brew that is specifically suited to their taste. A five-star rating is considered a "world classic," a four star is "a fine example of the style," a three-star brew is "enjoyable and well-produced," and one and two rating brews are considered average. The beers available at Archer Ale House come from all over the Europe and the United States including Belgium, Germany, Holland and England. Off-menu beer specials are also available.

Appetizers, soups and salads are available to snack on. For less hungry patrons there are — in the tradition of old England — pretzels for munching. There are daily chef specials and other dishes like Beer Sausage Pizza and oysters.

Written by Tyler Watson

About the Authors

Kimberly Baer

As a senior at Western Washington University with one quarter remaining, I am looking forward to wrapping up my college career and moving on to bigger and better things. I am studying Creative Writing and Photography, and hope to pursue both these interests in the future. Outside of school, I enjoy making artsy projects, exploring bookstores, and cooking extravagant foods.

I prefer rain to sun, fiction to poetry, fall to winter (especially in Bellingham). I love planning road trips—even if they are just for the afternoon—and taking afternoon naps. I hope to some day visit Italy, Norway, and Alaska and use these places as backdrops for future stories.

Glen Berry

As the Project Manager of Kulshan.com, Berry implements design elements, manages contributing authors, contributes creative content and provides digital photography for the site. Berry is also the graphic designer of Kulshan.com.

Berry brings with him an expertise in design and site building, having a number of professional web sites to his credit. An award winning filmmaker, Berry comes from a background in film production and post production as well as 35mm still photography. Berry is also the creator of the popular and successful "film underground" network of filmmaking web sites.

A fourth generation resident of Washington State, Berry was born and raised in Bellingham, Washington and is an active member of the community. Berry is a former Eagle Scout and serves as a member of the Board of the Whatcom Film Association. Berry graduated from Bellingham High School, attended Western Washington University and received a Bachelor of Arts degree in Film from Montana State University.

When he is not staring at a computer screen, Berry also enjoys basketball, road trips, cooking from scratch and Kurt Vonnegut.

Wayne Berry

Wayne Walter Berry founded Sign Me Up Marketing in 1996. As with all start-up companies, Berry is responsible for the design, product development, and strategy that drives this innovative high-tech company.

As a former Microsoft design engineer, and the director of development for FreeShop, Berry's expertise includes software design, development, marketing and online business. The web site he created as a hobby to assist in distributing information to Active Server Page developers became his first product, 15 Seconds. The recent sale of 15 Seconds to Internet.com allowed Berry time to develop his latest product, XBuilder, and Kulshan.com, a community web-site for his hometown, Bellingham, Washington.

The Bellingham native graduated from Bellingham High School, and Western Washington University with a BS in computer science. Berry is the author of three books, ActiveX Unleashed Programming, Windows Registry Guide, and Special Edition - Using Microsoft Internet Information Server 4.0. A popular and respected speaker, Berry recently spoke to the Professional ASP Developers Conference in Denver and has been invited to speak to an international ASP conference in Sweden.

Ken Brierly

As the ambiguous title of Community Editor may imply, Ken Brierly wears many hats. With Kulshan.com since November 1998, Brierly, 23, writes site content, copy edits and compiles event information. Aside from working with Web-based content, his career goal is to spend several years fine-tuning his skill in journalism, before turning those comprehensive experiences toward the classroom as a college journalism professor. In terms of practical experience, he has already gained well-rounded credentials in the field.

As a product of Western Washington University's journalism department, Brierly established himself as a solid news and feature writer. Eventually, he was hired as news editor, and later, managing editor of the campus publication, The Western Front. Instead of confinement to campus publications, Brierly branched out. He currently covers prep sports for The Bellingham Herald, and is a writer, copy editor and former contributing editor for Filter.98225, a local arts and entertainment magazine. He copy edited a non-fiction book for The Charles Press, and served as a reporter, photographer and presentation editor for The Baton, the first official publication of the National Wilderness Conference.

He is an avid sports fan and has not impressed former girlfriends with his habit of watching the same episode of Sportscenter, back-to-back. He enjoys fishing, hiking, jet skiing and mountain biking.

Shelagh Considine

A West Coast person, to be sure, Shelagh is a boat person. While all her sailing was done in the South Pacific and the Caribbean, she has lived aboard old freighters in Sausalito in its heyday. (When it was filled with artists and writers.) Born in Vancouver, B.C. she has lived from there to San Diego on this continent. She has been in Bellingham just a year. A sculptor and craftsperson, an interest in the arts has lead her to Computer Graphics. She is a reader. Of everything, ask any librarian. I guess if she gets talked into accolades, she'll add them later.

Dave Erickson

David Erickson was born a long time ago in Edmonds, Washington. He is a graduate of the University of Washington with a Bachelors Degree in Landscape Architecture and Washington State University with a Masters Degree in Sport and Recreation Management. This would explain his general state of confusion around Apple Cup time. David lives in Ferndale with his wife, Deanne, son, Michael, and two mentally challenged cats, C.J. and Taylor. In 1997, David took up golf as a hobby and is regretting that decision ever since. He spends much of his free time in his workshop creating custom outdoor furniture, birdhouses and bird feeders. You may also find him voraciously reading historical novels, science fiction and mysteries or completing residential landscape designs and consultations. A strong advocate of parks and recreation, you may most likely find him snoozing under a tree at a park or at parks@nas.com.

Debra Exley

Having left a warm and safe and dry career in health care, I began to resculpt myself as a writer—a not so warm, definitely unsafe and questionable-as-careers-go sort of endeavor. Life forces gave a nod of approval though and flung the doors open hard and wide. Writing larks that have resulted in public recognition include author interviews, book reviews, book editing and personal interviews. Writing the content for web sites comes easily to me and is so satisfying, I now direct my talents toward that venue.

My speckled past includes the good fortune to live in some indisputable garden spots: the Monterey Peninsula of California, the front range of the grand state of Colorado and now Anacortes, Washington. There was a colorful patch of extended RV travel when with kayaks and bikes lashed to a green '78 truck, my partner Dan and I appeared something akin to the Clampets. We can enliven any drab dinner party with stories gained from our brief stint managing an RV park during that life period.

Life for me is best in the garden, on a hike with our center-of-the-universe dog Lucia, at the keyboard composing (language!) or when reading GREAT fiction by a SUPERB author. For Kulshan.com, I'll be the one out there on the trails, notepad in hand with an eye toward accessibility, and the large brown dog showing us all how life ought to be lived.

Hilary Higgins

After graduating from Oberlin College in the late 80s, I spent the next ten years living and working in Germany and enjoying many travel adventures all over Europe. My Scottish husband James and I have worked together on the Isle of Skye in northern Scotland; gone on busking tours in various countries; worked in Irish pubs and beer gardens in Regensburg, Germany; picked grapes in Burgundy, France. Before moving to the States in 97, we spent a year traveling around Europe in a VW bus with our floppy dog Huck Finn. Between my travels and working, I found time to study as a technical translator for German and English and have worked in that capacity in both Germany and the US. During our year in the van I also began a writing course for the London School of Journalism and wrote some travel articles while on the road. James and I moved to Bellingham from Wisconsin in January so I could accept a job with a small technical communications company. I also work as a translator and writer on a freelance basis. When I'm not stuck in front of a computer, I can be found exploring the back roads of Bellingham on my bike, hiking up Chuckanut Mountain with James and Huck, or playing ultimate Frisbee. After so much travel and moving around, we feel we couldn't have found a more beautiful place than Bellingham to hang up our traveling shoes for a while.

Bertha Marsau

Thirty years ago I made my first trip to Bellingham and fell in love with the place. My husband and I are from Bremerton, which means I've lived my whole life in Western Washington, with the exception of three years, when I was a student at Central Washington University in Ellensburg. Obtaining a BA Ed degree in Home Economics in 1975, I soon became a homemaker and volunteer in Whatcom County. We have two sons, Mike (19) and Brian (15).

My passion is community. I've volunteered with WSU Cooperative Extension as a Master Food Preserver/Food Safety Advisor for 16 years and ten years ago founded my own nonprofit charity, Northwest Braille Services. I free-lance as a Braille transcriber. An active member and Community Awareness chair for the Health Support Center, I just recently became a webmaster (December 1998) when I began developing a site for HSC, and have expanded it to include links to other nonprofit sites, and supportive pages for local artists and musicians. I have created two local email discussion lists: Whatcom_Nonprofits, and Whatcom_Webmasters, in hopes of opening communication between people in the local cyberspace. My most recent hobby has involved posting local events and announcements up on the Internet, while listening to my growing collection of local CDs.

Rob Olason

A "forty-something" life-long native of Whatcom County, Rob Olason lives in Fairhaven with his wife and two elementary school aged children. An avid film buff, Rob ran the Picture Show Theatre in the 1980's and currently owns and manages Trek Video in Fairhaven. With a wide range of interests, Rob has dabbled in writing, filmmaking, animation, theatre and photography. The Internet is a current passion. Rob has created and maintains Web sites for Trek Video and The Bellingham Theatre Guild.

Tanya Perkins

I am a recent arrival to the Pacific Northwest, having moved here 10 months ago from Lexington, Kentucky. I am originally from Alberta, Canada, but marriage to an American led to life in the States. I majored in paralegal science in college and worked as a paralegal, primarily in business law, up until the birth of my daughter 16 months ago. Since then, motherhood has been a full time job, with no regrets. Favorite pastimes are travelling, hiking, wine tasting, and sewing. Since moving to Bellingham and buying an old farmhouse, renovating has also been added to the list.

Dave Shepherd

Dave Shepherd is a 27-year-old senior at Western Washington University, teetering on the brink of being thrust back into the real world. His only defense: an English major, a plethora of minors (journalism, Russian language, archaeology), the ability to use "plethora" in a sentence and write in third person, cat-like ninja skills and a complete lack of shame.

With this stunning array of tools, he hopes to go write stuff and get paid for it, preferably in exotic lands where he speaks the language (Australia, Russia, Spain, South America, Colorado). If you're an employer, contact him at Hemmingway2000@hotmail.com. If you're a fan, adore him at hemingway2000@hotmail.com. If you have complaints, he's currently between computers, so has no email address; telephones give him the "willies." Dave appreciates you caring who wrote this stuff!

Nancy Steele

My passions are music and writing, two closely related areas. A pianist since childhood, I moved to Bellingham in 1980 to pursue my dream of earning a music degree in piano performance. After years of practicing and more practicing, I successfully fulfilled that dream, graduating in 1985.

Since then, I have taught piano, composed music, performed locally for holiday crafts fairs, weddings, and other special events, and recorded "Shimmering Waters", a CD and cassette of soothing flute and piano music featuring Sage Waters, flutist and myself (please check out www.bima.com/ for more information).

I became interested in writing while working part-time for my spouse, Rick Steele, a Bellingham CPA who owns his own business. Inspired by writing client spotlights for the firm's quarterly newsletter, I sought additional writing opportunities. Several years later, I began writing classical music reviews and advances for the Bellingham Herald. Following that, I wrote press releases and newsletter articles for the Mount Baker Theatre; start-up business profiles and features for Business Pulse Magazine; classical music performances (and other topics) for the Every Other Weekly; and press releases, newsletters, and brochures for a variety of small business owners.

I've started my own business, Personalized Writing Service, which offers clients copy editing, proofreading, newsletter, brochure and Website content writing; promotional and marketing materials and press releases.

Tyler Watson

Tyler Watson is currently the entertainment editor of Western Washington University's newspaper, The Western Front. More notably, he is a freelance writer and has written highly acclaimed magazine articles such as, "One Toke Over the Line: The Story of Vancouver's Slow Drug Death" and "The Nation and the Knife," a look at America's obsession with excessive plastic surgery. Watson is now doing research for his next piece, entitled "Blood, Sweat and Beers: Human Wreckage on White Sand Beach," a story about Florida's spring break party migration.

Watson, who is in his mid-twenties, was born in Vancouver, British Columbia, and has traveled throughout the world reeking havoc and leaving broken hearts in his wake. He has been deported from five countries for what international officials have called, "crimes of love."